Journeys

Journeys:

An Introductory
Guide to Jewish
Mysticism

WILLIAM E. KAUFMAN

Bloch Publishing Company
New York

Acknowledgements

For permission to reprint exerpts from their works, the author is indebted to:

The Boston Globe: Article on Temple Emanuel of Lowell, Massachusetts by Jerry Ackerman. Appeared December 22, 1978. Reprinted by permission of the Boston Globe.

Citadel Press: *The Way Of Man* by Martin Buber. Copyright © 1966. Reprinted by permission of Citadel Press.

Doubleday & Co: *Kabbalah: The Way Of The Jewish Mystic* by Perle Epstein. Copyright © 1978 by Perle Epstein. Reprinted by permission of Doubleday & Co.

Horizon Press: *Hasidism And Modern Man* by Martin Buber. Copyright © 1958. Reprinted by permission of the publisher. *The Tales Of Rabbi Nachman* by Martin Buber. Copyright © 1956. Reprinted by permission of the publisher.

David McKay Co: *Nine Gates To The Chassidic Mysteries* by Jiri Langer. Trans. Stephen Jolly. Copyright © 1961. Reprinted by permission of David McKay Co.

Macmillan Inc: *Between Man And Man* by Martin Buber. Trans. Ronald Gregor Smith. Copyright © 1965. Reprinted by permission of the publisher.

Mockingbird Books: *Life After Life* by Dr. Raymond A. Moody, Jr. Reprinted by permission of Mockingbird Books Inc.
New Directions Publishing Corp: *The Wisdom Of The Jewish Mystics* by Allen Unterman. Copyright © 1976 by Allen Unterman. Reprinted by permission of New Directions.

Paulist Press: *Abraham Isaac Kook-The Lights Of Penitence, The Moral Principles, Lights Of Holiness, Essays, Letters, And Poems.* Trans. and introduction by Ben Zion Bokser. Copyright © 1978 by Ben Zion Bokser. Reprinted by permission of the publisher.

To my wife Nathalie, for her love, and to our children, Ari and Beth, for asking the right questions.

Contents

Foreword

In this volume, Rabbi William E. Kaufman offers a lucid survey of the evolution of Jewish mysticism. His presentation is directed to the questing adult and also toward those youth of our day who feel that the physical world, with all its joys and charms, is not the whole of existence. They are truly "seekers of the Lord", though only a tiny fraction would consciously describe their restless longing in religious rhetoric. Some are at times drawn to exotic and fantastic cults, especially when they are unaware of the mystical dimension in historic Judaism.

It is interesting that Dr. Kaufman, a serious student of Jewish philosophy, was drawn toward the study of mysticism. In this endeavor, he exemplifies not merely the contemporary mood of our time, but in a deeper sense, he demonstrates the inner unity of an authentic rationalism and a healthy mysticism.

The mainstream of Judaism has always been both rationalistic and mystical. Seen from the standpoint of Aristotelian philosophy, Judaism appeared to be mystical in its insistence that "the beginning of wisdom is reverence for the Lord". Seen from the vantage point of most religions, especially most versions of Christianity, Judaism appeared to be rationalistic.

Consider the famous debate of Nahmanides, one of the architects of Jewish mysticism, versus Pablo Christiani in 1263 at Barcelona. "The core of the dispute among us," Nahmanides maintained, "is not the concept of the Messiah. . .but the crux of the issue and the reason for the argument between Jews and Christians is the fact that you impute to the Deity things which are exceedingly repugnant. . .the thought of a Jew and a man cannot tolerate such a belief; hence you argue for naught and your words are wasted, for this is the essence of our dispute." (*Sefer Haviknah Lehvramban*, 12)

1

Authentic Judaism, argued Nahmanides, is fully in agreement with the logic of the human mind, with "the thought of a Jew and a man," and thereby enshrines the unity of the rational and the mystical. The quest of spiritual wholeness may be identified as the creative impulse in Judaism.

The so-called Biblical "prophetizers" (*mitnabim*) were ecstatics, who impressed the populace by their asceticism, their fervor and their mystical prowess. The true prophets, on the other hand, blended their mystical visions with self-criticism, self-judgment and self-dedication. The Holy Scriptures contain "the Torah of the priests, the word of the prophet, the counsel of the wise". (Jeremiah 18:18). In the *Ethics of the Fathers*, we are cautioned, "If there is no reverence, there is no wisdom; if there is no wisdom, there is no reverence."

While the quest of wholeness was ignored at certain times by the legalistic authorities, the Jewish philosophers remained true to it, from Saadia to Hermann Cohen and from Judah Halevi to Martin Buber. Even if it may not contain answers to the mysteries of life, our mystical tradition exemplifies diverse pathways on the quest for wholeness — wholeness of the individual within himself, wholeness between the individual and his historic community, between that community and redeemed mankind, between all things and God.

Rabbi Kaufman speaks of a "series of journeys". Man was designed to move toward goals that he can dimly sense but never reach. A person's wholeness embraces ideals, aspirations and sentiments that lead far beyond his concrete self. Hence, growth is the primary law of the human spirit. Does Jewish mysticism in our day convey this feeling of "Divine discontent"? Religious experience humbles even more than it exalts. It deepens our awareness of our human ignorance and it inspires our endeavors to "learn from all men".

As Dr. Kaufman points out, students of mysticism should approach their subject with a full awareness of its profound ambivalence. An introduction to mysticism must warn the reader, as Kaufman does, against the many perversions of the mystical quest, which are forms of escape from reality. Let me mention four:

First, escape from the near, the familiar, the rational into the remote, the absurd and the exotic. To the unconscious, the absurd is a symbolic defiance of the real world. Hence, the popularity of strange rites and "dark speech" to those who think they are rejected by the common sense community. Some people may have to retreat temporarily from the entanglements of reality, in order to recover their bearings. At times, we need to step back in order to leap ahead. But transitions can become traps. The Talmudic tale of "the four who entered paradise", discussed in this volume, is intended to warn would-be mystics.

Second, escape into dogmatism. In authentic religious life, faith and doubt are two sides of the outreach of the soul toward the Divine mystery. In many versions of "orthodox" dogmatism, doubt is rejected as the seduction of the devil, and a living faith is hardened into so many dogmas, designed to protect the faithful from the anguish of life. It is good to hope, to dream, even to "build castles in the air", but it is silly to attempt to live in them.

Third, escape into sacred ethnicism. One way of retaining popular approval while abandoning reality is to follow the road of collective self-deification. This type of ethnocentric mysticism views the individual as fallible, but the instinct of the masses or the folk as sure, deep and unerring. Echoes of this tendency, duly softened by the extreme intensity of the humanistic tradition in Judaism, can be perceived in Kabbalah, in the early Buber and in Kook. Those who are not deeply rooted in a powerful ethical tradition are easily corraled into mass movements, where they check their rational faculties at the gate in return for the exalted feeling of being "saved".

Fourth, the danger of revived paganism. We hear much today of the virtues of returning to nature, of celebrating the rhythms of life, of the earth as the feminine deity, the Great Mother, the Moon and the Sun. Nature is, of course, the teacher of all. But there is all the difference in the world between the celebration of life in paganism and the celebration of the spirit in Judaism. Spirit is the cutting edge of the Divine in man. Spirit is human nature at its highest — it is the majestic imperative of the ethical, the aesthetic, the intellectual and the holy.

In brief, the mystical quest is a significant element in the structure of the good life. But it is not a magical talisman. The great virtue of William E. Kaufman's book is that it takes this mystical quest seriously and treats it as an essential part of spiritual growth without belittling rationality or assigning it a subordinate role.

JACOB B. AGUS
BALTIMORE, MD.

Preface

The first stirrings of my interest in mysticism occurred during an adult education seminar I was teaching on the subject of Maimonides. During the evening, I mentioned that on an intellectual level, I found Maimonides' abstract concept of God attractive. Dr. Saul A. Wittes, an aesthetically inclined member of the group, then asked me if I believed in a personal God. After some moments of reflection, I said, "In my heart of hearts, I believe, but I cannot justify it intellectually or rationally."

"Not everything needs a rational justification," the doctor replied. "You ought to study mysticism."

Shortly thereafter, I was invited to teach a course on Jewish mysticism at Clark University, Worcester, Massachusetts. The subject has held immense fascination for me ever since. I have continually sought in Jewish mysticism "another way of knowing" the Divine, the "reasons of the heart" for religious belief. But my proclivity toward rationalism was constantly in the way.

Then I met Jan Schoenheimer, Managing Editor at Bloch Publishing Company. She opened up an entire new world to me: the inner world, the world of the psyche, the dimension of the soul. She led me to the realization that our rigid distinctions between subject and object—our vaunted linear rationality—is itself merely a human construction. Modern science itself, she showed me, discloses the relativity of so called "objective reality" to the mind of the perceiver. In brief, in our frequent discussions, Jan pointed out to me the power of the human mind, the beauty of the soul, and the oneness of the universe. In our conversations, and based on my experience in teaching Jewish mysticism, we realized that a basic introductory guide to Jewish mysticism was an absolute necessity.

Jan introduced me to Laura Schwartz, who fascinated me by her quest for spirituality. She stimulated my interest in contemporary developments in Jewish mysticism—such as the Havurah movement—and spiritual figures such as Rabbi Everett Gendler. I am grateful to both Jan and Laura for their editorial suggestions.

I wish to thank Rabbi Jacob Agus not only for his interest in the manuscript and his constant inspiration, but also for kindly consenting to write the foreword for this book. I am grateful to Rabbi Everett Gendler for sharing his spiritual understanding with me. I am also indebted to Rabbi Levi Yitzchak Horowitz, the Bostoner Rebbe for the time he spent with me and his fascinating discussions of contemporary Hasidism. Also, I must thank Rabbi Yehoshua Laufer, for his enlightening comments on Lubavicher Hasidism and for his permission for me to attend his *Tanya* class at Brown University Hillel. I wish to point out that the views expressed by his students do not necessarily reflect the point of view of Lubavicher Hasidism.

Also, I want to express my gratitude to Professor Nahum Sarna of Brandeis University, for his helpful suggestions regarding the interpretation of key passages in the Biblical book of Ezekiel. Dr. Stanley Nash, Professor of Hebrew Literature at the Hebrew Union College—Jewish Institute of Religion and Professor Thomas Schwartz of the University of Texas at Austin also provided helpful suggestions concerning the manuscript.

A thank you to Elliot Schwartz, Director of the Bureau of Jewish Education of Rhode Island, for his careful reading of the manuscript and his pedagogical suggestions.

The encouragement of the members of the Congregation B'nai Israel, Woonsocket, Rhode Island and of the Congregation Agudas Achim, San Antonio, Texas is greatly appreciated. I would like to thank Jeffrey and Richard Brenner, Lowell Gilbert, and Jill and Peter Tedeschi. Our stimulating discussions helped with many aspects of this manuscript. Words cannot express my gratitude to Mrs. Karin Begum for her careful reading of the manuscript and the example of her personal quest for spirituality.

I want to extend special thanks to Charles Bloch of Bloch Publishing Company for his most valuable assistance in all aspects of the development of this book. And I also want to express my special gratitude to Melvin Powers of Hollywood, California and Israel Medoff and Samuel J. Medoff of Woonsocket, Rhode Island for their special interest in this project.

Sandra Whipple and Agnes Gibbons typed the manuscript. I am thankful to them for their patience and accuracy.

Most of all, I wish to thank my dear wife, Nathalie, and our children, Ari and Beth—to whom this book is dedicated—for their love that enabled me to persevere in the writing of this work.

W.K.

Introduction

Sweet melodies will I sing to Thee
And hymns compose,
For my soul yearns for Thee,
My soul yearns for Thy Presence,
To know the mystery of Thy Being.[1]

The foregoing words are the opening verses of the "Hymn of Glory", a mystical poem recited in many synagogues on Sabbaths and festivals. The author of this prayer, according to tradition, was Rabbi Judah of Regensburg, a medieval philosopher and poet, saint and mystic, who died in 1217. In this hymn, we find the fundamental motif of mysticism: the yearning to experience the presence of God. To the mystic, God is not an abstract entity, whose existence is merely a matter of philosophical speculation. Rather, the mystic's innermost self—his soul—is stirred by the love of God, and he seeks to know through experience the mystery of God's being. Accordingly, a mystic is an individual "who has been favored with an immediate, and to him real, experience of the divine, of ultimate reality, or who at least strives to attain such experience. His experience may come to him through sudden illumination, or it may be the result of long and often elaborate preparations."[2]

The mystic is aware of the difficulty of his search: he knows that there is a vast gulf separating finite man from infinite God. For this reason, when a mystic does succeed in penetrating the veil—experiencing the Divine—it is an experience that cannot be easily conveyed or described in ordinary language. Thus, mystical experiences are often said to be "ineffable" or inexpressible except through the use of paradoxes, metaphors and poetic expressions.

Consider, for example, these famous lines of the mystical poet William Blake:

To see the world in a grain of sand
And a heaven in a wild flower,
Hold infinity in the palm of your hand,
And eternity in an hour.[3]

A grain of sand or a flower can be a stimulus for a mystical experience, for the mystic often sees nature as a mystery that points to an infinite and eternal Being—to God.

Despite the difficulty of articulating the content of a mystical experience, there is a feeling communicated by the genuine mystic that he knows something about the mystery of our existence that we don't know. Such "knowledge" is clearly worlds apart from "scientific" knowledge. It is private, not public; that is, it is based on the experience of a single individual and is thus unrepeatable, whereas scientific knowledge is based on observational or other criteria agreed upon by the scientific community which can be tested or repeated, for example, in a laboratory.

To examine whether or not we are actually justified in speaking of a mystical way of knowing—a type of knowing other than scientific knowledge—is one of the purposes of this book.

Journeys

We have noted that some mystical experiences come through "sudden illumination", while others are the result of long and often elaborate preparations. It is also important to note that when we define a mystical experience as an "experience of the divine, of ultimate reality", that "divine" or "ultimate" is seen differently in various religions, and the mystic way to the Divine is culturally conditioned by the symbols of a specific religion. Whereas a Jew having a mystical vision might see a Torah, a Christian, by contrast, would be more likely to see a cross, or a vision of Jesus. Such a Christian vision of Jesus offers an excellent example of a mystical experience of "sudden illumination."

The Christian apostle Paul (originally Saul), on his journey to

10

Damascus, had an experience of sudden illumination: "light from heaven blazes around him, and falling on the ground, he hears a voice saying 'Saul, Saul, why persecutest thou me?' "[4] Saul's experience of Jesus, who was to represent *his* ultimate reality, was a mystical experience that came through sudden illumination, described graphically as "light from heaven blazing around him."

Other mystical experiences are the result of "long and often elaborate preparations." The mystic, we recall, is not only someone who has been favored with a mystical experience but also one who "strives to attain such experience."

How does one strive to attain mystical experiences? What kind of preparations are involved?

Mystics throughout the ages have described the spiritual life as a journey or pilgrimage. The Sufi—a Moslem mystic—for example, who sets out to seek God calls himself a traveler; he advances by slow stages along a "path."[5] He is embarking on an inner journey, an interior ascent. Recall the opening words of the "Hymn of Glory," and the reference to the yearning of the soul to enter into contact with God. By an "inner journey," we mean an ascent of the soul—the inner self—to a higher level of spirituality. Specifically, it is an ascent to that level at which the soul is "pure" enough or "godly" enough to experience the highest level of reality—the Divine.

The stages of a Jewish inner journey to holiness and spirituality are described in the following passage of the *Mishnah*, the compendium of the Oral Law edited by Rabbi Judah the Prince in the second century C.E.:

> R. [Rabbi] Phineas b. [son of] Jair says: Heedfulness leads to cleanliness, and cleanliness leads to purity, and purity leads to abstinence, and abstinence leads to holiness, and holiness leads to humility and humility leads to the shunning of sin, and the shunning of sin leads to saintliness, and saintliness leads to [the gift of] the Holy Spirit, and the Holy Spirit leads to the resurrection of the dead.[6]

Each stage on this "ladder of virtues" leads to a higher plateau, until finally this "inner journey" culminates in the gift of the Holy

Spirit: a level of spirituality in which the soul experiences a closeness to God and an intimation of its immortality.

Another Jewish mystical journey is reflected in *The Book of Direction to the Duties of the Heart*[7] by the medieval Jewish philosopher Bahya ben Joseph ibn Pakuda (ca. 1080). Bahya's *Duties of the Heart*, as it is popularly known, is a devotional work. Influenced by Sufi mysticism, Bahya describes in his book a mystic journey—a path through various "gates" in order to experience closeness to God. Each chapter of the *Duties of the Heart* represents a "gate"—an inner state of the soul, a level of the spiritual life.

The first chapter—the first gate—represents the necessity for intellectual understanding of the unity of God. The second chapter is a meditation upon Creation and God's abundant grace as manifested therein. Equipped with the necessary cognitive understanding of God's unity, and His wisdom and grace as manifested in Creation, the seeker is now ready to ascend the spiritual rungs of the ladder toward total devotion and love of God. Thus the third chapter relates our obligation of obedience to God; the fourth centers on reliance upon God alone; the fifth upon pure devotion of all acts to God above; the sixth upon humility before God; the seventh on repentance; the eighth on self-reckoning concerning one's duties toward God; and the ninth on asceticism or self-denial. The tenth and culminating chapter, or gate, is "the true love of God." Here, then, are the steps of a medieval Jewish mystical journey—from intellectual recognition of the unity of God through emotional trust in God and self-purification (humility, repentance, self-reckoning or self-examination and abstinence) to culmination in love of God and contact of the soul with God.

Bahya's mystical journey was one of many "inner ascents" in the history of Jewish mysticism.

The purpose of the present book is to trace the steps of the most significant Jewish mystical journeys. Among the questions we shall examine are: What did the Jewish mystics seek? What were the stages of their journey? What knowledge did they claim to achieve? What insights did they attain into the nature and workings of the Divine, into man and his place in the universe, and into the "soul" and its ultimate destiny in "heaven"?

We shall divide this study of Jewish mystical journeys into four parts.

First, we will discuss the early Jewish mystics whose quest was largely based on Ezekiel's vision of God's throne in heaven. We shall also describe the Jewish mystical concept of heaven.

The second part explains the ways in which medieval Jewish mystics thought about and meditated upon God.

In the third part, we describe the Jewish mystics' ideas about man: his place in the universe, his relation to God, the concept of the *Messiah*—the ideal leader, and the *Zaddik*—the perfected man.

Part four discusses the effect of Jewish mystical journeys on earth. We show how Jewish mysticism has become a vital form of Judaism in the community and in the modern world. We explore some contemporary options open to the modern Jew in search of a mystical way.

The concept of mystical journeys is not merely an ancient or medieval notion. It is also thoroughly contemporary. Dag Hammarskjold, the late Secretary-General of the United Nations, was, in his private life, a man with marked mystical tendencies. In his autobiographical work, *Markings*—a kind of spiritual diary—he wrote:

> *The longest journey is the journey inwards.*
> *Of him who has chosen his destiny.*
> *Who has started upon his quest*
> *For the source of his being . . .* [8]

As we begin to trace Jewish mystical journeys, we hope that the reader will also embark upon a journey inwards, in quest of the source of his or her being.

A Parable

As we embark upon this journey, the reader may be skeptical. Is it possible for a modern individual to reach the ultimate destination of the journey: to make contact with God? The following parable represents the skepticism of many moderns about mystical experiences.

Suppose a tourist was invited to visit the emperor of a foreign country. Upon entering the emperor's palace, a servant showed him the emperor's beautiful gardens, his chambers and his incomparable art collection. After seeing these things, the tourist expressed a wish to see the emperor.

The servant then said, "You cannot meet the emperor. But you can believe that he exists. You see his gardens, his chambers, his art collection. They aren't here by accident. They indicate that the emperor exists. Furthermore, you can take my word for it. I have met the emperor."

The tourist has not met the emperor. He has not "made contact." He infers that the emperor exists on the basis of seeing his gardens, his chambers, his art collection. His problem is whether or not to believe that the servant has actually met the emperor.

The tourist in this story represents the attitude of most moderns to God. With the exception of a minority of atheists and agnostics, the majority of people profess a belief in God. Their belief, however, is rarely based on direct contact with God. It is, in most cases, an inference from the created world to the existence of a Creator: most people tend to believe that the universe did not just happen. They infer from the fact that the world exists, that its Creator—a supreme Being or God—exists.

Most scientifically oriented people are skeptical of accounts in the Bible in which individuals do make contact with God. Like the tourist who was uncertain about whether the servant had met the emperor, most Americans with a scientific, rationalistic orientation are uncertain whether to give credence to the testimony of figures in the Bible who claimed to hear the "voice" of God or to see "visions" of God. The only way to transcend these doubts is to explore in greater depth our own spiritual experiences and relate them to these testimonies.

Tradition plays a major role in Judaism. The thinking Jew must take some position with regard to the testimony of the Bible regarding encounters with God. And since the basis of the Jewish tradition is the revelation of God's *Torah* at Mount Sinai, wherein the Bible alleges that the entire people of Israel at that time heard the "voice" of God, the Jew who takes Judaism seriously must form some notion of what happened at Sinai.

Kabbalah

The study of the Jewish mystical tradition in conjunction with our own inner journeys can illuminate the minds not only of Jews but of people of all faiths who are seeking a contemporary understanding of their ancient faith. The Jewish mystical tradition is called *Kabbalah*, which comes from a Hebrew root meaning "to receive." The word *Kabbalah* means "that which has been received." *Kabbalah* is the record of the wisdom and teachings which were received and handed down by Jewish mystics throughout the ages. *Kabbalists*, or Jewish mystics, believe that answers to many difficult questions about man, the world and God can be found in this tradition.

The beginnings of the Jewish mystical tradition are rooted in the prophet Ezekiel's vision of God, described in chapter one of the Biblical book of Ezekiel. Ezekiel's vision of God was not the only instance of an encounter with God in the Bible. Moses, for example, had many such encounters; we have noted that the entire Jewish people under Moses' leadership "encountered" the Divine at Mount Sinai. Nevertheless, there was something new about the way Ezekiel described his vision that made it different from the experience of other prophets, including even Moses. What was this new element in Ezekiel's encounter? Ezekiel gave a bold, vivid and detailed description of God *as he experienced Him*. This was the novel element in Ezekiel's vision and it was, perhaps, for this reason that *Maaseh Merkabah*—the "account of the chariot" (Ezekiel's vision of the Divine throne)—became a foundation stone of *Kabbalah*; a point of departure for the Jewish mystical tradition.

Our first journey into Jewish mysticism, therefore, takes us back to the sixth century B.C.E.—to the prophet Ezekiel and his vision of God.

15

Reflection

Throughout our inquiry, it is important to bear in mind that mystical experiences are not merely confined to the historical past. Mircea Eliade, an authority in the history of religion, has maintained that "particularly coherent mystical experiences are possible at any and every degree of civilization and of religious situation."[9] A great deal, however, depends upon the belief system of a given individual or culture. At a time when scientific rationalism is the dominant cultural attitude, mystical experiences are hardly noticed. In this last half of the twentieth century, however, it is generally recognized that science cannot give us absolute truth; there is no Archimedean point of absolute certainty. Signs of a new openness and a willingness to give credence to mystical experiences are becoming evident.

What is needed, therefore, in order to embark upon a study of these Jewish mystical journeys is an attitude of openness: openness to the possibility of mystical experience as a viable option for the contemporary Jew, receptivity to new insights and new ways of seeing the world, and the awareness of new ways of viewing the journey to self-discovery—which some say is really the journey to God as the source of our being. "The longest journey is the journey inwards. . . . "[10] But a journey, no matter how long, begins with but a single step. The single first step is openness to otherness: to the sacred, to the extraordinary; above all, to the mystery which surrounds our existence.

Part One

HEAVEN

1

Ezekiel's Vision of God

Early Jewish mysticism had its source in the prophet Ezekiel's account of his vision of God. In the opening chapter of the Biblical book of Ezekiel, the prophet tells of his experience by the banks of the river Chebar in Babylonia. Ezekiel relates: "As I was among the captives by the river Chebar, the heavens were opened, and I saw visions of God."[1] Ezekiel goes on to describe his vision of God's chariot and throne. This event came to be known by Jewish mystics as *Maaseh Merkabah*—"the account of the chariot."

What did Ezekiel see? And can we believe that what he saw was a vision of God? To answer these questions, we must first find out who Ezekiel was and how he became a captive in Babylonia.

Who Was Ezekiel?

The book of Ezekiel tells us little about the prophet's personal life. What we do know is that he was the son of Buzi, born of the priestly family of Zadok. It is also known that he was married and that his wife died suddenly. A most important fact was that Ezekiel was one of those Judeans who were taken captive by the Babylonians along with Jehoiachin, the king, in 597 B.C.E.

In the year 586 B.C.E., the first Temple in Jerusalem was destroyed by the Babylonians. The Jews became exiles; almost all of them in Babylonia. Why then was Ezekiel taken eleven years earlier?

Ezekiel was one of 8,000 Jews taken captive with King Jehoiachin. It was the policy of the Babylonians to take first, people they could make the best use of: "the court and nobles, the

19

priests and scholars, the military leaders, and the skilled crafts-men—what today would be called technicians. These were people that Babylon could use and Judah could not spare."[2]

When the exiles came to Babylonia, they were homesick. Thus it is related in the first verse of Psalm 137: "By the rivers of Babylon, there we sat down, yea, we wept, when we remembered Zion."[3]

Many of the exiled Jews wished to return to the Holy Land im-mediately. False prophets arose who promised that God would soon destroy Babylonia and bring them home.

Ezekiel knew that these hopes were false. Unlike the false proph-ets who told the people what they wanted to hear, Ezekiel spoke the truth. He foresaw the destruction of the Temple. His proph-ecy was proved true, for the Temple *was* destroyed in 586 B.C.E. Ezekiel also warned that the Exile would be long, and he advised his fellow captives to adjust to life in Babylonia.

How did Ezekiel know these things? Being a prophet means having unique understanding. The Hebrew prophets saw themselves as instruments of God. The Hebrew word for proph-et—*Navi*—means "a spokesman for God." When a Hebrew prophet proclaimed "Thus saith the Lord," he believed that he was a messenger of God, inspired by God.

Ezekiel was not only a prophet. He was also a priest, trained for service in the Temple in Jerusalem. As a priest, he had to be con-cerned with details. Every ritual connected with the Temple ser-vice had to be carried out carefully.

It was his eye for detail that made Ezekiel's vision of God unique. His was the most detailed and explicit description of a vision of God ever given by a Hebrew prophet. For this reason, his account became the source of early Jewish mysticism.

Ezekiel's Vision

Ezekiel's task as spiritual leader of the Jewish exiles in Babylonia was a difficult one. The exiles believed that the Temple in Jerusalem was God's dwelling place. How could they worship God in a strange land? Ezekiel had to teach them that God could be worshipped even in Babylonia. He had to make it absolutely clear to them that God was withdrawing His presence from the Temple in Jerusalem as a prelude to its destruction, that they could worship God without a Temple; for God was present in Babylonia—indeed, could be present anywhere. According to the Bible, Ezekiel's conviction about the truth of his vision came directly from God: " . . . the word of the Lord came expressly unto Ezekiel the priest, the son of Buzi, in the land of the Chaldeans [Babylonians] by the river Chebar; and the hand of the Lord was there upon him."[4] Ezekiel felt seized by God, grasped by the overwhelming power of God, the "hand of the Lord." This is why he was convinced that what he saw was a vision of God. Biblical scholars believe that Ezekiel's vision took place in the year 593 or 592 B.C.E.[5] Here is part of Ezekiel's description of what he saw (for the complete text of Ezekiel's vision, see Appendix I, p. 197)

I looked, and, behold, a stormy wind came from the north, a great cloud, with fire flashing through it, and a radiance round about it, while out of the midst of it gleamed something with a luster like that of shining metal.

Out of the midst of it stood forth the likeness of four living creatures, and this was their appearance: their form was like that of a man. Each, however, had four faces and four wings.

Over the heads of the creatures was the likeness of a vault, and it glittered like transparent ice, and was stretched forth above their heads. Under the vault one pair of their wings touched those of the next creature, while the other pair covered the body. When they moved, the sound of their wings sounded to me like the sound of mighty waters, or like the voice of the Almighty.

Above the vault that was over their heads was the likeness of a throne, colored like sapphire; and upon the likeness of the throne was a likeness like that of a man sitting upon it.

From the appearance of his loins upward I saw something with a luster like that of a shining metal; and from the appearance of his loins downward I saw something resembling fire, with a radiance round about it, resembling the bow that appears in the clouds on a rainy day.

Such was the likeness of the glory of the Lord, as it appeared to me.
And when I saw it, I fell upon my face.[6]

It is difficult to understand Ezekiel's vision. What Ezekiel saw
was mysterious and awe-inspiring. For many centuries, Jewish
mystics thought about Ezekiel's vision. They believed that if they
could understand Ezekiel's vision, they could discover God. They
believed that what Ezekiel said about God was true.

What did Ezekiel actually see? What were the key elements in
Ezekiel's vision?

Ezekiel said that the heavens were opened and that he saw visions of God. To Ezekiel, God's dwelling place was in heaven.
What he saw was the heavenly throne of God.

Ezekiel felt a stormy wind from the north, saw a great cloud
with fire flashing through it. The wind from the north was a symbol of the impending invasion of Jerusalem by the Babylonians
from the north. The cloud and the fire were symbols of the Divine
presence.

Another part of Ezekiel's vision describes four winged creatures
pulling a *Merkabah*, or chariot, on wheels whose rims were
covered with eyes. These four creatures were composite figures,
their faces having four separate countenances: the face of a man in
front, the face of a lion on the right side, that of an ox on the left
side, and that of an eagle behind. The man, lion, ox, and eagle—all
sovereign in their realm—were symbols of God's sovereignty; the
wheels represented God's omnipresence; the eyes, God's
omniscience.

Over the chariot, Ezekiel saw a vault or platform upon which
rested something like a throne. And upon the likeness of the
throne, he saw something like a man sitting upon it. This appearance, Ezekiel said, was "the likeness of the glory of the
Lord."[7] When he saw this, Ezekiel was overcome by awe of God.

Reflection

The key word in Ezekiel's vision is the word "likeness." Ezckiel
did not claim to "see" exactly what God is. By using the word

"likeness", Ezekiel was saying that his vision of God as the One who sits on the throne in heaven was a mystery even to him. This is a common feature of mystical experiences. Mystical experiences can only be hinted at or suggested in words. What really happens in such experiences is a mystery.

Most important was Ezekiel's reaction to his vision: "And when I saw it, I fell upon my face."[8] This expresses his awe and reverence, his feeling of self-abasement and fear in the presence of God—the great and holy King.[9]

It is this feeling of Ezekiel's that makes it possible to believe that what he saw was really a vision of God, as God appeared to him. Ezekiel was responding to the holy and the sacred—to a Power beyond this world. But he responded in his own way, and his image of God was based upon his own needs and his own experiences.

Ezekiel's vision of God was thus *his* idea, *his* image, of God. He saw only a likeness of God. He came as close to God as any man ever did, but God's Being was still a mystery to him. It was this mystery that the early Jewish mystics sought to understand.

2

The Journey to Heaven

The earliest group of Jewish mystics were known as *Merkabah* mystics—explorers of God's chariot (*Merkabah*). They tried to understand the mystery of Ezekiel's vision of God. Ezekiel had described God's chariot and throne. He had claimed to see the "likeness" of God upon His throne in heaven. These early Jewish mystics wanted to know what Ezekiel saw. They wished to see the *Merkabah* themselves.

To do this, they placed themselves in a trance. They believed that while in a trance, they could leave their bodies and ascend to heaven. The destination of their journey was God's chariot and throne in heaven.

Who were these early Jewish mystics? Why did they make this journey to heaven? How did they accomplish it? What happened on this journey? How did they visualize heaven? And was their journey real or imaginary?

The Early Jewish Mystics
These first Jewish mystics lived in Palestine in the first and second centuries of the Common Era. They belonged to a group studying with Rabbi Yohanan ben Zakkai.

Rabbi Yohanan ben Zakkai lived in the first century c.e. In the year 70 c.e., the second Temple in Jerusalem was destroyed by the Romans. Ben Zakkai's greatest achievement was to gain permission from the Romans to found an academy at Yavneh. This academy became the spiritual center of Judaism after the Temple in Jerusalem was destroyed.

Ezekiel's vision of God's chariot in motion underscored how God withdrew His presence from the first Temple before the Babylonians destroyed it in 586 B.C.E. and yet was present everywhere. Ezekiel's vision of God leaving the Temple in His chariot helped Rabbi Yohanan and his students to understand what was happening when the second Temple was destroyed. This was one reason why Yohanan and his students thought deeply about Ezekiel's experience.

But there was another reason, too. Rabbi Yohanan and his students wanted to know what heaven was like. This kind of knowledge was offered by a new way of thinking called Gnosticism. Why did they seek such knowledge?

Gnosticism

Jews have always been influenced by the cultures in which they lived. To understand why certain Jewish Rabbis in the first and second centuries wanted to know what heaven was like, it is important to know what was happening at this time in history.

People often become interested in heaven when life on earth is difficult and troubled. Palestine, during much of the first and second centuries, was a place of suffering. At this time, Palestine was ruled by Rome. In the year 44 C.E., the whole of Palestine was annexed as Roman territory and placed under the rule of Roman officials called procurators. For twenty-two years these procurators held sway and made life miserable for the people.

These procurators were greedy. They stole public and private funds. They plundered whole cities, and many communities were ruined. By the end of the year 67 C.E., the whole of the north of Palestine was brought under total subjection by the Romans.[1] Roman tyranny finally led to the destruction of the Temple in Jerusalem in the year 70 C.E.

It was natural for people to wish to escape from this world. The desire to escape from this world to another world—to heaven—gave rise to the idea of salvation. Salvation is the belief that true happiness is to be found not on earth but in another world—in heaven. New religions arose promising such salvation.

People looked for a Messiah—a miraculous leader to save them. Many believed that the end of the world was at hand, and that a Messiah would bring a new world. The new religion of Christianity had arisen, claiming that Jesus of Nazareth was the Messiah. Jesus won many followers to his cause when he said, "My kingdom is not of this world." This promise of salvation in heaven exerted a powerful effect on the masses.

But there were other religions of salvation besides Christianity. A most interesting one was Gnosticism. Some of the ideas of this religion influenced early Jewish mysticism.[2]

"Gnosticism" comes from a Greek word, *gnosis*, meaning knowledge. The purpose of Gnosticism was to impart knowledge about heaven and to provide instructions concerning how to get to heaven and reach the true God.

The Gnostic religion was one of dualism: the Gnostics believed in two gods. The true God, who is totally good, is in heaven. This world, the earth, was created by a lesser God, who is not good at all.

To the Gnostics, the earth was a prison; a dark and gloomy place. In contrast, heaven is a place of light and goodness. Why, then, are we here on earth and how can we get to heaven?

According to Gnosticism, the lesser God, who created the earth, left its rule to evil beings called Archons. The Archons rule the world and try to prevent man from reaching heaven and the true God.

But man can outwit the Archons by receiving knowledge of the true God, and by learning the way to reach heaven from a mysterious messenger sent by this true God. The seeker must prepare himself by learning secret names and formulas. Having learned them, he is ready for the instructions of God's mysterious messenger concerning the way to heaven.

The Jewish *Merkabah* mystics thought of the journey to heaven in terms of Ezekiel's vision of God's throne and chariot. Because the idea of the journey to heaven was a Gnostic idea, the thought of these early mystics is also known as Jewish Gnosticism. This does not mean that many Jewish Gnostics came to believe in two gods—an idea contrary to Judaism's fundamental principle of monotheism, or belief in One God. But one Jewish Gnostic, Rabbi Elisha ben Abuyah, did fall prey to the belief in two gods partly because of what happened on his journey to heaven. He was one of the four Rabbis whose unusual voyage to heaven is described in the Talmud. The secret tradition of Merkabah mysticism, taught by Rabbi Yohanan ben Zakkai, was transmitted to these four Rabbis.

The Journey of the Four Rabbis

The early Jewish mystics made the journey to heaven by putting themselves in a trance. In this trance state, they believed that they could leave their bodies. This kind of trance led to a mystical experience called *ecstasy*: a feeling of being outside one's body.

In this state of ecstasy, they believed that they could journey to heaven. How did they visualize heaven?

They saw heaven as consisting of seven firmaments. To be precise, they believed that there were seven heavens. In the seventh heaven, they believed there were seven palaces. And if one could reach the seventh heavenly palace in the seventh heaven, one would see God's chariot and throne.

How did they place themselves in such a trance? Here is a description of the procedure used by a Jewish mystic:

> He must fast a number of days and lay his head between his knees and whisper many hymns and songs whose texts are known from tradition. Then he perceives the interior and the chambers, as if he saw the seven palaces with his own eyes, and it is as though he entered one palace after the other and saw what is there.[3]

This is the way the early Jewish mystics embarked on their journey. They fasted a number of days. They placed their heads between their knees, a physical position inducing a trance. They sang hymns from their tradition, such as the songs of the holy creatures who carry God's chariot and throne.

Consider one part of these procedures: they fasted for a number of days. You probably know what it feels like after you fast for one full day on Yom Kippur, the Day of Atonement. But think of what it would be like, and what would happen to someone if he fasted for a full week! Depriving oneself of food for so long would weaken one's body and perhaps put one in a state of mind where he might see visions.

Obviously, a person does not go through such exercises unless he believes that the result of doing this is of the utmost importance to him. To four Rabbis who lived at the end of the first and beginning of the second centuries c.e., the most important thing was the search for truth. They wanted to understand the Great Mystery: God. They knew that in their ordinary state of mind they could not see God. In their ordinary state of mind, they could not visualize God's chariot and throne as described by Ezekiel:

> The four creatures . . . and each had four faces . . . wheels within wheels . . . and their rims were full of eyes . . . a firmament like the color of terrible ice . . . the likeness of a throne, as the appearance of a sapphire stone . . . the likeness as the appearance of a man . . . colored like the bow that is in the cloud in the day of rain.[4]

These four Rabbis realized that they could only understand these mysterious words of Ezekiel if they put themselves in a trance, and in a state of ecstasy journeyed to heaven.

Who were these four Rabbis? And what happened on their journey?

The leading scholar among these Rabbis was Rabbi Akiba. Born in the year 40 c.e., Akiba rose from humble beginnings to become one of the greatest Rabbis of all time.[5] A tall, bald man of great physical stature, Akiba spent his first forty years as an ignorant peasant shepherd. He was saved from a life of ignorance by Rachel, the woman who was to become his wife. Rachel saw the potential greatness of his mind, and inspired him to begin studying Hebrew. Once he began to study, he showed himself to be a towering intellect. He mastered the Law, and was the author of a collection of laws which later became the *Mishnah*. Through his ingenuity, he was able to find a Biblical basis for virtually every

law. But he was not only a student and a teacher. He was a
staunch defender of the right of the Jew to study Torah. He
defended this right even when the Romans issued a decree forbid-
ding the Jews to study. Defying this decree, Rabbi Akiba was put
to death by the Romans. Rabbi Akiba died the death of a martyr
for his God and for his people in 132 c.e.

Akiba was not only a master of Jewish law. There was another
side to his character—a mystical one. It was this mystical aspect of
Akiba's personality that led him to organize a mystical group consisting of three other Rabbis: ben Azzai, ben Zoma, and Elisha ben
Abuyah.

Ben Azzai, whose full name was Simeon, son of Azzai, was so
devoted to the study of the Torah that he never married. The
Torah was his bride. He was a very sensitive soul and possessed a
saintly character. His most famous saying was: " . . . the reward of
a good deed is a good deed."⁶

Ben Zoma, whose full name was also Simeon, son of Zoma, was
a master of *Midrash:* the art of explaining and interpreting verses
of Scripture. To be a master of this art required an active imagination. It was his imagination that led him to ask questions that
could not be answered. He would think endlessly about what happened when the world was created. But his imagination was not
balanced by an ability to reason.

Elisha ben Abuyah was the son of a wealthy landowner. He was
not as devoted to the study of the Torah as were the three other
Rabbis. His real interest lay elsewhere: in Greek philosophy and
the strange ideas of Gnosticism. Because he had doubts about the
principles of Judaism, Elisha was on the verge of losing his faith
and becoming a heretic or non-believer (thus becoming known as
Aber—"another person").

By being familiar with the character of these four Rabbis, we
can better understand what happened to each of them. Here is a
description of their journey:

> Once four Talmudic sages went on the mystical journey to *Pardes*.
> They were Ben Azzai, Ben Zoma, *Aber* [the name by which Elisha ben

Abuyah was known], and Rabbi Akiba. Rabbi Akiba said to them: When you reach the stones of pure marble be careful not to say 'Water, water,' for it is written 'He who speaks falsehood cannot stand before My eyes.' Ben Azzai gazed and died; Ben Zoma gazed and went mad; *Aher* cut the plants [i.e., became a heretic]; Rabbi Akiba came out in peace.[7]

It is very difficult to understand this strange passage completely. Scholars of the Talmud have been puzzled by it for centuries. It is possible, however, to understand some of its meaning.

What are the key-words of this passage? They are: *Pardes; Aher;* stones of pure marble; water, water; gazed; cut the plants.

The Hebrew word *Pardes* (literally "garden" or "orchard"), like the English word Paradise, refers to the Heavenly Paradise or heaven. The point at issue is whether this journey to heaven was real or imaginary. Interpreters of the Talmud differ on this question. The commentator Rashi claims that the four Rabbis actually ascended to heaven. Another commentator, Rabbi Hananel, explained that it only appeared to them that they entered heaven: the whole incident was only a vision.

Whether the journey was real or imaginary, it was a shattering experience for all but Rabbi Akiba. Ben Azzai gazed and died, Ben Zoma gazed and went mad, and *Aher* became a heretic.

What did they gaze at? What were the stones of pure marble? Why were they instructed not to say 'water, water'?

The dangers of the journey were enormous. The chief danger presented itself at the sixth palace. This is how it is described:

At the gate of the sixth palace it seemed as though hundreds of thousands of waves of water were storming against him, and yet there was not a drop of water, only the ethereal glitter of the marble plates with which the palace was tessellated [adorned].[8]

This is what the Rabbis gazed at and what caused terrible things to happen to three of them. What they encountered were the angels of the sixth palace. The angels of the sixth palace, like the Archons in the Gnostic religion, created obstacles on the ascent to heaven. They tried to frighten the seekers by making it seem as if the marble stones or plates of the palace were waves of water. Three of the four Rabbis were unable to master this obstacle. Only Rabbi Akiba realized that this was merely a test, and so he warned the others: "When you arrive at the stones of pure marble, do not think it is water. The angels are only trying to deceive you and frighten you." But the illusion created by the angels was too strong an obstacle for Ben Azzai, Ben Zoma, and *Aher*.

Can what happened to these Rabbis be explained? It appears that only Rabbi Akiba was fully prepared for this mystical journey. Rabbi Akiba possessed both a powerful mind and a stable personality. He came back in peace. Ben Azzai was too sensitive a person to emerge from the journey alive. Ben Zoma's too-active imagination led him astray. He became insane as a result of the experience. Elisha ben Abuyah was already known as *Aher*—another person—because he had become like another person: drawn away from Judaism toward Greek philosophy and Gnosticism. This experience merely pushed him over the edge. He became a heretic, rejecting the principles of Judaism. He cut the plants; he denied the roots, the foundations of Judaism. He adopted the Gnostic belief in two gods, denying Judaism's root principle of the One God.

The meaning of this mystical journey emerges from the experiences of the four Rabbis. Rabbi Akiba came back in peace because he was the only one of the four who was prepared for it. This passage in the Talmud is a warning to those who seek mystical experiences: "Do not go on a mystical journey unless you feel that you are stable enough to return from it with your mind and body intact."

This warning is especially important for our time. People today have used drugs, such as LSD, to induce mystical experiences. One should not "try out" any kind of mystical experience unless he is sure he can "come back" from it with a sound and healthy mind. This is the lesson we learn from the journey of the four Rabbis. Only Rabbi Akiba who went up informed and prepared came back unhurt.

Reflection

Why did the angels wish to prevent the Rabbis from seeing the vision of God's throne and chariot in the seventh palace of the seventh heaven? Perhaps the angels wished to guard God's presence. Perhaps they felt that only they, and not man, were entitled to see God, the Holy King. And perhaps the entire experience was recorded to express the words of God in the Bible: "for man shall not see Me and live."[9]

But what about Rabbi Akiba? How much did he see? The Talmud relates:

> Rabbi Akiba went up unhurt and went down unhurt . . . And Rabbi Akiba too the ministering angels sought to thrust away; but the Holy One, Blessed be He [God] said to them: "Let this elder be, for he is worthy to avail himself of My glory."[10]

The angels thus tried to prevent Rabbi Akiba's ascent to God, but they failed. They failed because God wished to show Rabbi Akiba His glory.

Did Rabbi Akiba actually "see" God? Notice carefully what the Talmud says: God showed Rabbi Akiba His *glory*.

Like Ezekiel, Rabbi Akiba saw a "likeness" of God; he saw God's glory. God appeared to him as a king upon a throne.

But Akiba did not actually "see" God Himself; for according to Judaism, no man can see God and live.

The way Akiba journeyed to God and his vision of God's glory show us how Jewish mystics at this time thought about God. They thought of God as far away, remote. They saw a great distance between themselves and God.

The journey to heaven can be thought of as a symbol of the great difference between man and God. God is like a Holy King on a throne in heaven. This is an image of God who is far away from man, different from man and very difficult to approach. Later Jewish mystics felt that God was not so far away. They felt He could be approached on earth as well as in heaven.

Was the journey of the four Rabbis real or imaginary? Rashi

thought it was real. Rabbi Hananel thought it was imaginary. The important thing is the effect this journey had on the four Rabbis; the difference it made in their lives. To the mystic, a thought, a dream, or an idea in the imagination can be the beginning of a journey to heaven.

But whether the journey itself is real or imaginary, it is a journey only to be taken by a stable, well-informed person. Mysticism is an adventure interesting to all, but open only to some—to those who have powerful minds and stable personalities. Such a person was Rabbi Akiba, the Jewish mystic who survived the journey to heaven.

3

The Zohar

The journey of the Rabbis was an attempt by four sages to enter heaven during their lifetime. One of these sages, Ben Azzai, died during this journey. What happened to him after his death? Did his soul live on? Did he see heaven more vividly in death than in life? How did Jewish mystics conceive of the soul and life after death? Did they believe that all souls go directly to heaven when people die?

These are the kinds of questions that are discussed in the most famous book of Jewish mysticism—the *Zohar*. Before we examine what the *Zohar* says about life after death, let us first find out what kind of book it is, the meaning of its title and who wrote it.

A Mystical Commentary

The *Zohar* is a mystical commentary on the Bible. Many of the great books in Jewish literature are commentaries. Most of the Talmud, for example, is a commentary.

The Talmud consists of the *Mishnah* and the *Gemara*. The *Mishnah* is a collection of Jewish law, learning and ethics compiled and edited at the beginning of the third century by Rabbi Judah the Prince. The *Gemara* (from the Aramaic word "to learn") is a commentary on the *Mishnah*, and forms the largest portion of the Talmud.

Why was such a commentary necessary? Judaism has passed through many stages of development. As laws were discussed, they were continually being viewed in new ways and applied to new problems and situations in the life of the Jews.[1]

The foundation of Judaism is the Bible. The Bible contains not only laws, but also narratives and poetry. Jews always tried to live by the Bible and to apply its teachings to new situations as times changed. So the Bible, like the Talmud, needed commentary and interpretation.

The most famous commentary on the Bible was that of Rashi, an acronym for Rabbi Schlomo Yitzhaki, who lived in France in the eleventh century. What Rashi tried to do was to make the Bible easier to understand.

The *Zohar* was also written in the form of a commentary on the Bible. But it was not like Rashi's commentary. Its purpose was not to make the Bible easier to understand, but rather to find in the Bible the secrets of the universe: the mysterious truth about God, the soul, heaven and creation. This commentary was a search for the secret meaning of the words of the Bible.

For example, the very first sentence in the Bible reads: "In the beginning, God created the heaven and the earth." (Genesis 1:1) The author of the *Zohar* believed that if he could understand the secret, hidden meaning of the Hebrew word *Bereshit*—"in the beginning"—he would solve the mystery of what happened before creation. This secret, hidden meaning of the words of the Bible was called, in Hebrew, *Sod.*

The Meaning of "Zohar"

Since the author of the *Zohar* was interested in the subject of life after death, it was natural for him to search the Bible for hints about heaven. There are very few references in the Bible to life after death. But there is a verse from the Biblical book of Daniel which clearly voices this belief:

> And many of them that sleep in the dust of the earth shall awake, some to everlasting life . . . And they that are wise shall shine as the brightness of the firmament.[2]

The Hebrew word for brightness, in this verse, is the word *Zohar.* To suggest the radiance of the righteous and wise souls in heaven, and the brilliant light of the presence of God, the author chose the word *Zohar* as the title of his book.

Bright light is a frequent element in mystical experience. Recently studies have been made about the mystical experiences of dying persons. In one of these studies, Dr. Raymond A. Moody emphasizes the symbol of light:

> What is perhaps the most incredible common element in the accounts [of dying persons] I have studied, and is certainly the element which has the most profound effect upon the individual, is the encounter with a very bright light. Typically, at its first appearance this light is dim, but it rapidly gets brighter until it reaches an unearthly brilliance . . . .
>
> Despite the light's unusual manifestation, however, not one person has expressed any doubt whatsoever that it was a being, a being of light. Not only that, it is a personal being. It has a very definite personality. The love and warmth which emanate from this being to the dying person are utterly beyond words, and he feels completely surrounded by it and taken up in it, completely at ease and accepted in the presence of this being.[3]

This being of light, according to Dr. Moody, was interpreted by some dying persons as an angel, by others as the presence of God Himself; most often the being of light appears to the dying person in accordance with his belief system.

According to the *Zohar*, at the center of the universe is an "innermost light"[4] of a brilliance beyond comprehension. In the *Zohar*, as well as in modern accounts, bright light is a symbol of the presence of God.

Who Wrote the Zohar?

One of the students of Rabbi Akiba was Rabbi Simeon ben Yohai. Like Rabbi Akiba, Simeon defied Rome. Because of his rebellious attitude toward the Roman Empire, the Romans sentenced him to death. According to a legend in the Talmud, Simeon and his son hid in a cave for thirteen years to escape the Roman decree.[5] During these years, the legend tells us, great mysteries were revealed to him from heaven.

After he departed from the cave, and was no longer in danger from the Romans, he founded an academy at Meron. According to Jewish tradition, he died there on *Lag Ba-Omer*. For centuries, Jews have memorialized him yearly on the Festival of *Lag Ba-Omer* by visiting his tomb.

For a long time, it was believed that Rabbi Simeon ben Yohai wrote the *Zohar*. The *Zohar*, it was said, was the record of the mysteries that were revealed to him in the cave where he and his son hid for thirteen years.

Modern scholars, however, find it difficult to believe that Rabbi Simeon ben Yohai actually wrote the *Zohar*. There are a number of reasons why scholars believe that he could not have done so.

Rabbi Simeon ben Yohai lived in Palestine in the first half of the second century. But the language of the *Zohar* is not the language Rabbi Simeon and his friends would have used. Medieval Hebrew expressions and inauthentic Aramaic words are used which would have been unknown to Rabbi Simeon. Furthermore, the descriptions of Palestine in the *Zohar* indicate that the author had never been there. They sound more like descriptions of Spain than of Palestine. And finally, there is evidence that the author used thirteenth century Kabbalistic writings in the composition of his book.[6]

All of these facts indicate that the *Zohar* was written by a Spanish Kabbalist in the thirteenth century. Most scholars believe that the *Zohar* was written and first circulated in the latter part of the thirteenth century by the Kabbalist Moses ben Shemtob de Leon, who lived until 1290 in the little town of Guadalajara, Castile, in Spain.[7] Why, then, did Moses de Leon not claim to be the author of the *Zohar* himself? Why did he ascribe its authorship to Rabbi Simeon ben Yohai?

Moses de Leon was reputed to have said, "If I told people that I am the author, they would pay no attention. . . . But now that they hear that I am copying the book *Zohar* which Simeon ben Yohai wrote under the inspiration of the holy spirit . . . "[8] people will be more interested in it. Moses de Leon therefore told this story: The *Zohar* was hidden in a cave, the very same cave Simeon ben Yohai and his son hid in for thirteen years. There the medieval Hebrew sage Nahmanides, on his arrival in the Holy Land, discovered it. Nahmanides sent the book to his son in Catalonia, Spain. But a wind carried it away and brought it to a certain place in Aragon, Spain, where it fell into his [de Leon's] hands.[9]

The evidence indicates that Moses de Leon himself was the author of the *Zohar*. Why did he write it? Moses de Leon was originally a follower of the philosophy of Moses Maimonides, the great twelfth century author of *The Guide of the Perplexed*. But gradually de Leon was attracted to the study of *Kabbalah*. He realized that philosophy, and its attempt to give a reasonable explanation of why Jews should observe the commandments, did not lead to greater religious enthusiasm. On the other hand, *Kabbalah*, and its idea that observance of the commandments was a mysterious ritual that had an effect upon God, could stir the people to greater piety. Moses de Leon was correct. It took two centuries for the *Zohar* to become popular. But from the years 1500 to 1800, the *Zohar* was considered a book equal in religious authority to the Bible and the Talmud.[10] It had a tremendous appeal for the Jewish masses. What were the ideas in the *Zohar* that made it so popular?

The Theme of the Zohar

The main theme of the *Zohar* states that our ordinary world on earth is only a reflection of a higher spiritual world in heaven.[11] Our world on earth, the "lower world," is patterned after heaven, the "upper" world. This is how the *Zohar* expresses this idea:

> Now God has made the lower world after the pattern of the upper world, and all the arrangements laid down by David and Solomon, and by all the true prophets were after the supernal [heavenly] pattern. Observe that in the same manner as there are watches of the night on earth, so are there in heaven relays of angels who sing praises to their Master and intone hymns continually; they all stand ranged in rows, facing each other, and producing one harmony of song and praise.[12]

Not only is the lower world patterned after the upper world; both worlds interact and affect each other. Thus the *Zohar* says that every human action on earth calls forth a corresponding action in heaven: "Thus if a man does kindness on earth, he awakens [God's] lovingkindness above."[13] By the same token, if a man does cruel things on earth, this arouses God's wrath in heaven.

This idea is known as the concept of correspondences:[14] there is a world above (heaven) and a world below (earth). What man does on earth affects what God does in heaven. And what God does in heaven affects man on earth.

The idea here that so appealed to the Jewish masses was the important role man played in the world. The Biblical concept of man's creation in the image of God was taken very seriously by the *Zohar*. What man does has a powerful effect on the world and on God. If man observes God's commandments, he can bring about greater harmony between the upper and lower worlds, thus enabling God's mercy to flow freely. In contrast, when man sins, he causes a separation between the two worlds, and arouses the stern judgment of God.

Thus, in the *Zohar*, the traditional Jewish concept that man and God are partners was taken one step further. According to the *Zohar*, God actually needs man's assistance to make earth a better place, to make earth more like heaven.

Life After Death

What does the *Zohar* say about life after death? According to the *Zohar*, every person has a soul. The soul is that part of each person which is immortal—that lives forever. The soul comes from God before birth and returns to God after death. The task of each person in life is to keep his soul as pure as possible by doing good deeds and refraining from doing evil.

There is a lovely passage in the *Zohar*, which describes the journey of the soul and its destiny:

At the time the Holy One, be blessed [God], was about to create the world, he decided to fashion all the souls which would in due course be dealt out to the children of men, and each soul was formed into the exact outline of the body she was destined to tenant. Scrutinizing each, he saw that among them some would fall into evil ways in the world. Each one in its due time the Holy One, be blessed, bade come to him, and then said: Go now, descend into this and this place, into this and this body.

Yet often enough the soul would reply: Lord of the world, I am content to remain in this realm [heaven] and have no wish to depart to some other, where I shall . . . become stained.

Whereupon the Holy One, be blessed, would reply: Thy destiny is, and has been from the day of thy forming, to go into that world.

Then the soul, realizing it could not disobey, would unwillingly descend and come into this world.

The Torah, counsel of the entire world, saw this, and cried to mankind: Behold, see how the Holy One, be blessed, takes pity on you! Without cost, he has sent to you his costly pearl, that you may use it in this world, and it is the holy soul.

. . . How much heed should a man take lest he wander in a crooked path in this world! For if he shall have evidenced his worthiness in this world, having watched over his soul with every precaution, then the Holy One, be blessed, will be greatly content with him, and daily speak his praise before the supernal [heavenly] family, in this wise: See the holy son who is mine in that world below! Behold his deeds and the probity of his ways.

And when such a soul departs from this world, pure, bright, unblemished, the Holy One, be blessed, daily causes her to shine with a host of radiances . . . A palace which is known as the Palace of Love sits amidst a vast rock, a most secret firmament. Here in this place the treasures of the King are kept, and all his kisses of love. Every soul loved by the Holy One, be blessed, enters into that palace . . . The Lord discerns each holy soul, and taking each in turn to himself, embraces and fondles her.[15]

In this passage, the soul is pictured as lovingly pleading with God to remain in heaven so as not to risk becoming impure on earth. But God commands each soul to take up its mission on earth. The Torah, God's teaching, considered the blueprint for the good life, is personified and pictured as urging man to guard his holy soul. Those souls that return to God unblemished are thought of as entering God's palace in heaven, there to be embraced and loved by Him. This is what Jewish mystics believe happened to the saintly soul of Ben Azzai.

But what about those souls that do not return unblemished? What about the souls of those who did not live righteous lives on earth, and who died without repenting for their sins?

Another passage in the *Zohar* describes the journey of such a soul and its destiny:

> At first the soul is taken to a spot called Ben-hinnom, so called because it is the interior of *Gehinnom*, where souls are cleansed and purified before they enter the Lower Paradise. Two angel messengers stand at the gate of Paradise and call aloud to the chieftains who have charge of that spot in *Gehinnom*, summoning them to receive that soul, and during the whole process of purification they continue to utter aloud repeatedly the word "Hinnom". When the process is completed, the chieftains take the soul out of *Gehinnom* and lead it to the gate of Paradise, and say to the angel messengers standing there: 'Hinnom [here they are], behold, here is the soul that has come out pure and white. . . .''
>
> A second ordeal has to be undergone by the soul on its passage from Lower Paradise to Upper Paradise; for while in Lower Paradise it is not yet entirely purged of the materialities of this world, so as to be fit to ascend on high. They thus pass it through the 'river of fire' from which it emerges completely purified and so comes before the presence of the Sovereign of the Universe beautified in every respect. Also the rays of celestial [heavenly] light afford it healing. This is its final stage. At that stage the souls stand garbed in their raiment and adorned in their crowns before their Maker. Happy is the portion of the righteous in this world and in the world to come.[16]

Just as the universe, according to the *Zohar*, was divided into a lower world and an upper world, so too does heaven consist of a lower Paradise and a higher Paradise. In the Jewish tradition, paradise is often referred to as *Gan Eden*, after the Garden of Eden which God planted here on earth and where He placed the first man, Adam, to taste of all the good the earth offered. The abode of the wicked, and the temporary abode of the doubtful souls who are neither righteous *nor* wicked, is called by the name *Gehinnom* in the Jewish tradition. The name *Gehinnom* comes from the name of an actual place on earth, a valley south of Jerusalem, *Ge-Ben-Hinnom*, the valley of the son of Hinnom, where according to Bible, wicked people sacrificed children to the pagan god Moloch. This accursed valley on earth became a fitting symbol for the abode of the wicked in the life beyond the grave.[17]

The *Zohar* in this passage is dealing with the fate of the doubtful souls—neither righteous nor wicked—whose merits and demerits were even when weighed in the balance. After death, such souls are taken to the interior of *Gehinnom*; where for twelve months there is a cleansing process, after which they are permitted to enter Heaven. This intermediate state after death for purging or purification of the soul was also known as purgatory. The *Zohar* describes the purging process, playing upon the Hebrew word "Hinnom"—which also means "here they are"—in this case, here are the souls that have been purged of their sins. When these souls pass through the final stage of purification—the river of fire—they are ready to come before God, the Holy King, in his heavenly palace.

In this way, the *Zohar* depicted life after death, the final destination of the journey of the soul. There is a tradition in Judaism that one says the Mourner's *Kaddish* for a deceased parent for eleven months, and not twelve, so as not to assume that the destiny of one's parent's soul is in doubt. Thus, Jewish belief, as expressed in the *Zohar*, influenced Jewish practice.

Reflection

The *Zohar*, we can see, is a strange and fascinating book. It tells us what many medieval Jews thought about heaven, about the soul, and about life after death. It became a very popular book for many reasons—because it exalted man's role in the universe, because it promised consolation for suffering on earth with bliss in heaven above and because it is a book rich in imagination.

How much truth is revealed in these imaginative journeys of the soul? It is for each person to decide what he or she thinks is meant by the "soul," by "heaven," by "life after death". Modern studies, like that of Dr. Raymond Moody, also shed light on these questions. The purpose of the *Zohar*, for us, is to stimulate us to think about these issues.

The *Zohar* also provides many interesting insights into the concept of God. These insights cluster about the exciting image of the *Sefirot*. It is to this subject that we now turn.

Part Two

GOD

4

The Sefirot

What can we really know about God? Can we imagine what God is like? Is God completely different from man? Are there ways in which God is similar to us?

Jewish mystics thought very deeply about this. The approach to these questions in the *Zohar* is that man cannot know what God is. But man can understand the powers God used to create the universe, to sustain it and to govern the people in it.

The mystery of what God really is the Jewish mystics called *Ein-Sof*. And God's mysterious powers were known as the *Sefirot*.

Ein-Sof

The word *Ein-Sof* means "infinite" or "without end." That which is infinite cannot be measured. It is greater than anything we can imagine.

The things we can definitely know about are things we can see, touch and measure. Consider, for example, the house in which you live. It has a definite size and shape. The rooms in your house can be measured. The living room, the bedroom, the basement—all have a definite length and width. Your house is finite: it is limited to a certain size and shape. It occupies a specific amount of space.

Consider the life-span of a human being. A person lives for a limited amount of time, a definite number of years. The life-span of a human being is a finite amount of time.

In contrast, God is not limited by space. God has no physical form. His Being extends without end. He is everywhere, and He

is greater than the entire universe. The universe may be like a
grain of sand to Him.

God is also not limited by time. God is eternal. He has always
existed and will always exist.

God is therefore not limited by space or time. This is what the
Jewish mystics meant when they called God *Ein-Sof*—the Being
"without end," the infinite Being. Because God is infinite, what
God really is cannot be imagined or conceived of by man. Since
what God really is remains a total mystery to man, the Kabbalists
spoke of this aspect of God as "the hidden God." What God
really is, to the Kabbalists, is hidden from man.

How then did the Kabbalists conceive of God creating the
world and man? How could God—who is infinite and totally different from the finite world and from man—create the universe
and the people in it? Why did God create man? And in creating
man, did God reveal anything about Himself?

In trying to answer these very difficult questions, the Kabbalists
believed that they discovered something very important about
God. What they discovered were the *Sefirot*.

The Sefirot

What actually were the *Sefirot*? To find out, let us begin by
examining what the word *"Sefirot"* means.

The Hebrew word *Sefirot* is the plural of the word *Sefirah*. The
word *Sefirah* comes from the Hebrew word *Sappir* (sapphire),
because the Kabbalists compared the brightness of God to that of a
sapphire stone.[1] They thought of the *Sefirot* as spheres of bright
light sent forth by God when He created the world.[2]

Many synonyms are used for the *Sefirot* in the *Zohar*: sayings,
names, lights, powers, crowns, qualities, stages, garments, mirrors,
shoots, sources and aspects.[3]

The Jewish mystics believed that there were ten *Sefirot*. The
number "ten" was considered a magical number in ancient times.
We see the significance of the number "ten" from a saying of the
Babylonian teacher Rav, who lived in the third century: "Ten are
the qualities with which the world has been created: wisdom, in-

sight, knowledge, force, appeal, power, justice, right, love and compassion."[4]

To the Kabbalists, the *Sefirot* were the ten powers or qualities within God that He used in creating the world. These powers were visualized as bright spheres of light. The *Zohar* says that the *Sefirot* "emanate" from the *Ein-Sof* in succession: "as if one candle were lit from another. . . ."[5] Moreover, they emanate in a specific order, beginning with *Kether*, or crown.

To "emanate" is to flow forth from a source. For example, we say that fragrance emanates from flowers. The *Sefirot* flow out of, or are drawn out from their source, like light from the sun, or water from a well. Why did God cause the *Sefirot* to flow forth?

God did not wish to remain totally hidden. He wanted to reveal parts or aspects of His life to man. One of the boldest ideas of Jewish mysticism is that "not only is God necessary to man but that man is also necessary to God, to the unfolding of His plans in the world."[6] God needed man. This is the reason, given by Jewish mystics, that the infinite God created the world and man. At a certain point, therefore, the hidden God turned outward to create the world.[7] He created the world by causing ten of His powers or *Sefirot* to emanate from Him.

But the Kabbalists believed that God not only created the world. He also sustains it and rules it. The *Sefirot*—the powers He used to create the universe—are also the powers He uses to govern the world and man. The *Sefirot* are like a chain joining God to the world and to man. They can also be compared to the rungs of a ladder. Each rung offers a different perception of God.

People think about God in different ways. God reveals different aspects of Himself to different people, depending upon their situation and their experiences in life. The *Midrash*, a commentary on the Torah, says:

> Come and see that the ways of God are not those of man. A mortal king cannot wage war and at the same time be a scribe and a teacher of little children, but God can do all these things. On the sea yesterday [at the Red Sea], He was like one waging war . . . and today at Revelation

[the giving of the Ten Commandments], He descended to teach His children Torah.[8]

The *Midrash* goes on to say that God revealed Himself "according to the power of each individual, according to the individual power of the young, the old, and the very small ones."[9]

The way God appears to each person thus depends upon their situation in life, their experiences, and their capacity to understand Him.

The Kabbalists emphasized this, too. The way each person thinks of the *Sefirot*, they said, depends upon his own perspective: "everything is from the perspective of those who receive."[10] The *Sefirot* can be compared to bottles of different colors through which water is poured.

The *Sefirot* or Divine powers are thus the different aspects of God as they appear to man. Like links of a chain, or rungs of a ladder, each *Sefirah* represents a stage on the way to God.

There are two ways of viewing the *Sefirot*. They can be viewed as stages of God's descent to man or as stages of man's ascent to God.

What are the names of the *Sefirot*? How are they related to each other? How did the Kabbalists meditate on them? And what do they teach us about God?

The Names of the Sefirot

The Kabbalists believed that the more we know about ourselves, the more we can know about God's powers. To be sure, we cannot know what God is: this is the mysterious *Ein-Sof*. But we can know God's powers: His ways, His aspects, His attributes. These we can know, they believed, because they are like qualities we possess—but on a far greater scale.

How do we describe a person? We do so by pointing out his attributes or qualities. Consider, for example, the statement: "Harry is a wise and good person." According to this sentence, the attributes of Harry are "wise" and "good."

During the Middle Ages, one of the problems Jewish philosophers thought about was the question of God's attributes. What qualities, they asked, does God possess? They tried to answer this question by thinking about the best qualities a human being can possess. God, they said, has these qualities, too. But when we say that "God is wise and good." it is not the same as saying that "Harry is wise and good." For God's wisdom and goodness are infinitely greater than Harry's wisdom and goodness.

The Jewish mystics also thought about the problem of God's attributes. But they did not just *think* about God's qualities. They *visualized* these qualities as spheres of bright lights. God's attributes came alive for them. They meditated on each attribute. What God's attributes were for the medieval Jewish philosophers, the *Sefirot* were for the medieval Jewish mystics.

Each *Sefirah* or attribute of God had a name. And each of these names referred to a creative power of God.

The first *Sefirah* was called *Kether* or crown. *Kether* was the name for the will of God.[11]

We cannot accomplish anything unless we exert our will. So too, when God began to create the world, His first step was to exert His will to create. Since God's will to create the world was His first act as King of the universe, it was called *Kether* or crown.

When we decide to do something, it is not enough just to exert our will. We must have in mind various ways or possibilities to accomplish what we want to do. A person is considered wise if he is able to foresee the possibilities of his actions.

Similarly, after God willed the creation of the world, He thought about the possible ways to bring the world into existence. The name for God's thought or wisdom was the second *Sefirah—Hokhmah* (wisdom).

Thought or wisdom is still not enough to accomplish anything. We must decide exactly how to accomplish it. After thinking about possible ways of acting, we must decide on a specific plan, a specific course of action. So, too, after God thought about the possible ways of creating the world, He decided on a specific plan. This ability to choose the best course of action among many possibilities is "understanding." The name for God's understanding was the third *Sefirah—Binah*.

Imagine a person who possessed *Hokhmah* without *Binah*. Such a person would be constantly thinking about the possibilities of everything without channelling his action in a specific direction. A man of *Hokhmah* without *Binah* would be like an absent-minded professor, unable to implement his ideas in any specific way. On the other hand, a person who possessed *Binah* without *Hokhmah* would be rigid—lacking in imagination and wisdom. The ideal person, therefore, would be balanced between *Hokhmah* and *Binah*.[12] To visualize this balance between *Hokhmah* and *Binah* in God, the Jewish mystics saw these two *Sefirot*, flowing from *Kether*, in this way:

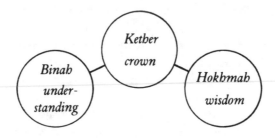

These first three *Sefirot* stand for the mind of God. They are the powers of God's mind which He used to plan His creation of the world.

How does God govern the world? What are the principles He uses to rule the world?

Consider an ideal king, a perfect ruler. If his rule was based on justice alone, his subjects would feel that he didn't care about them. But if his rule was based on mercy alone, his subjects would not respect him enough.

So, too, both God's mercy and justice were necessary for creation. If God used one without the other, the result would have been chaos. If God used mercy alone, the world would overflow with God's love. There would be no limits to anything. But if He used justice alone, man could not survive the rigors of God's judgment. Both justice and mercy were therefore necessary.[13]

The fourth *Sefirah* is *Hesed*—God's mercy or lovingkindness. God's mercy is balanced by *Din*—the fifth *Sefirah*. *Din* is God's power of stern judgment and punishment.

The harmony or balance between *Hesed* and *Din* is represented by the sixth *Sefirah*. This *Sefirah* is called *Tifereth* or beauty, since the harmony of *Hesed* and *Din*—like the harmony of fine music—makes us aware of beauty.

The Kabbalists visualized these three *Sefirot* in this way:

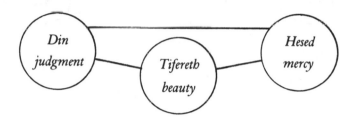

Unfortunately, these *Sefirot* are not always perfectly balanced. When man sins on earth, the Kabbalists believed, he upsets the harmony of God in heaven.

When the sins of men exceed their good deeds, *Din* or God's strict judgment is no longer balanced by *Hesed*—God's mercy. This is one reason that evil comes into the world. It is the result of the sins of man.

Notice that the Sefirah of *Din* is on the left. This left side of God is known as the *Sitra Ahra*—the "other" side of God—and is considered the source of evil. The *Sitra Ahra* was one of the ways the Kabbalists used to explain why there is evil in the world.

But when the good deeds of men balance or outweigh their sins, there is harmony in heaven. This harmony is represented by *Tifereth*—the sixth *Sefirah*.

Tifereth is not only the harmony of *Hesed* and *Din*. It also acts as a balance between the *Sefirot* above it, and those below it. To show how *Tifereth* acts as a balance, we can visualize the first six *Sefirot* in this way:

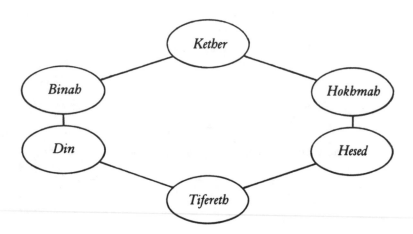

The first group of *Sefirot—Kether, Hokhmah,* and *Binah*—stands for the mind of God. They are considered the principles of the intellectual world.

The second group of *Sefirot—Hesed, Din* and *Tifereth*—stands for the principles God uses to rule the world. They are considered the principles of the moral world.

The third group of *Sefirot* stands for God's principles of ruling the natural, physical world.

The Kabbalists believed that God's powers had both male and female aspects. The male aspect was represented by the right side of the *Sefirot.* The female aspect was represented by the left side of the *Sefirot.*

The seventh *Sefirah, Netsah* or victory, stands for the male aspect of God's powers. It represents the power of nature to increase herself.

The eighth *Sefirah, Hod* or majesty, stands for the limiting aspect of nature. If nature only increased herself, without limitation, the result would be absolute chaos. The *Sefirah* of *Hod* therefore serves to limit *Netsah*.

The development of the *Sefirot*, we can see, is like a system of checks and balances. The right side stands for expansion and increase; the left side represents contraction and decrease. And the middle *Sefirot* represent the balance between them.

Thus the ninth *Sefirah*—balancing *Netsah* and *Hod*—represents the harmony of nature. This Sefirah is called *Yesod*, or "foundation". It is the life force—the foundation of nature, the balance of nature. These three *Sefirot* can be visualized in this way:

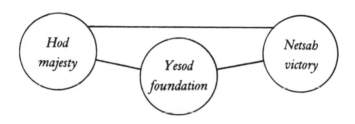

To the Kabbalists, one of the reasons God created the world and man was the special purpose He had in mind for the Jewish people. The Jewish people—the community of Israel—were to be His chosen people. The Kabbalists believed that God's love for the community of Israel was so great that He wished to reveal His presence to them.

The Kabbalists compared God's love for the Jewish people to the love of a king for a queen. The tenth *Sefirah—Malkuth* (kingdom) represented the union of God, the king, with His queen (the community of Israel). This *Sefirah* was also known as *Shekhinah*—God's presence. The union of God with the community of Israel was the climax of creation.

We can now visualize the ten *Sefirot* as they flow from the *Ein-Sof*:

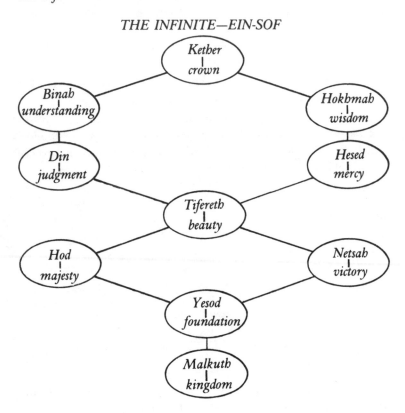

THE INFINITE—EIN-SOF

Kether
|
crown

Binah
|
understanding

Hokhmah
|
wisdom

Din
|
judgment

Hesed
|
mercy

Tifereth
|
beauty

Hod
|
majesty

Netsah
|
victory

Yesod
|
foundation

Malkuth
|
kingdom

The Kabbalists meditated on these *Sefirot*. They imagined them as a series of dancing lights against the branches of a tree.[14] Closing his eyes, the Kabbalist visualized each *Sefirah* vibrating with color, blazing with Hebrew letters:

Kether
Hokhmah
Binah
Hesed
Din

Tifereth
Netsah
Hod
Yesod
Malkuth

To the Kabbalist, each *Sefirah* took on a life of its own. He imagined them forming combinations with each other, illuminating each other, ascending and descending together.

By meditating on the *Sefirot*, the Kabbalists believed that they were linking themselves with God's creative powers, with the actual life of God as it poured forth in creation.

These medieval Kabbalists believed they understood more than the earlier Kabbalists, who had had a vision of God as a King upon a throne. They believed that they were actually linking themselves with the inner workings of God, as revealed in His creative powers. The old vision of God as King was only one of His aspects. They believed they could understand many more aspects of God, as represented by the ten *Sefirot*.

To the medieval Kabbalists, meditation on the *Sefirot* was a way to know the creative powers of God.

Reflection

What do the *Sefirot* teach us about God? Study of the *Sefirot* teaches us to think about God in terms of man's highest qualities, such as wisdom, understanding and mercy. Jews have always believed that when they treat their fellow man kindly, they are imitating God.

The Kabbalists thought of the *Sefirot* as the actual creative powers of God. Some of us may agree with the Kabbalists that these are the actual powers God uses to rule the world.

Some of us, on the other hand, may prefer to think of the *Sefirot* as symbols. A symbol is a word or thing used to express something intangible: something that cannot be seen, felt, or touched. Consider, for example, the sentence: "the lion is a symbol of courage." The word "lion" in this sentence is used to express an intangible idea: courage. Another symbol is the American flag. The flag represents the United States of America, and the idea of patriotism toward our country.

Symbols are used frequently in religion. In the prayer book, for example, God is often spoken of as "a rock." This does not mean that God has the physical properties of a rock. The word "rock" is rather a symbol of God's strength, and His ability to help us in time of trouble.

The *Sefirot* can be thought of as symbols of God. They are words and images the Kabbalists used to convey intangible ideas, such as God's wisdom and mercy.

But it is important to remember that to the Kabbalists, the *Sefirot* were not only symbols. They believed that the *Sefirot* were the actual powers God used to create this world, and to govern it. They believed that the *Sefirot* were the actual attributes of God.

The *Zohar* says: "Woe unto the man who should make bold to identify the Lord with any single attribute."[15] Study of the *Sefirot* teaches us that there are many qualities, many attributes of God. God appears differently to different people. It is a mistake to believe that any single idea of God is the only way to think about God.

There are actually many ways to think about God. Each *Sefirah* is a symbol of one of these ways. But even all of the *Sefirot*, taken together, do not describe all the aspects of God.

God is greater than all of the words we use to describe Him. This is why the Kabbalists said that the *Sefirot* are only aspects of God. The infinite greatness of God is the *Ein-Sof*, a mystery we cannot know.

5

A Medieval
Jewish Meditator

The most daring medieval Jewish mystic was Abraham Abulafia. Abulafia lived in the thirteenth century, the same century in which the *Zohar* was written. He was familiar with the descriptions of the *Sefirot* in the *Zohar*. But he felt that thinking about the *Sefirot* was only a prelude to a higher type of meditation. He believed he could go beyond the *Sefirot*, and could gain even more insight into God than the author of the *Zohar* did.

The method of meditation discussed in the *Zohar* was the "Path of the Sefirot." Abulafia's new method was called the "Path of the Names." It consisted of reflections on the names of God. The final stage of Abulafia's method was meditation on the holiest name of God. This name of God, according to ancient Jewish law, was only pronounced by the High Priest on the Day of Atonement in the Holy of Holies—the most sacred part of the ancient Temple. And Abraham Abulafia dared to meditate on this name!

Why was the holiest Hebrew name of God kept a secret? What gave Abulafia the courage to meditate on it? Did he feel that he was singled out by God to engage in this practice? If so, why did he think that he was given this unique role?

The Name of God

There are many names of God in the Hebrew Bible. Some of these are: *Elohim, El* and *Shaddai*.

The holiest name of God was known as the *Tetragrammaton*. *Tetragrammaton* is a Greek word meaning: "The name of four letters."

The four Hebrew letters of the holiest name of God are
יהוה, and are referred to in English as *YHWH*. *YHWH* is the
personal name of God in the Bible. It occurs 6,823 times in the
Hebrew text of the Bible.

The original pronunciation of the four letter Hebrew name of
God—*yod, hay, vav, hay*—has been lost due to strong Jewish disap-
proval of pronouncing God's name. This name was considered
too holy to be said aloud by anyone except the High Priest. In the
ancient past, people believed that the real name of their god held
secret powers. The Jews were afraid that if anyone other than the
High Priest mastered the absolutely correct way of saying "the
Name", this would lead to attempted use of this name for magical
purposes. Therefore, in Jewish practice, "the Name" was never
pronounced as written but as *Adonai*—meaning the Lord".

According to the Talmud, the only time the name *YHWH* was
pronounced was on Yom Kippur, the Day of Atonement. It was
pronounced then by the High Priest, in the "holy of holies" room
in the Temple, at the most sacred part of the Yom Kippur service.
The people standing outside the "holy of holies," in the Temple
court, heard "the Name" indistinctly. Only the High Priest had
mastered its pronunciation. The Talmud describes the reaction of
the people when they heard "the Name":

> When the priests and the people standing in the Temple court heard
> the Ineffable Name out of the mouth of the High Priest, they knelt
> and bowed down and fell on their faces and said: 'Blessed be the
> Name, the glory of whose kingdom is forever and ever.'[1]

According to the Talmud, the very sound of God's Ineffable
[not to be spoken or expressed] Name filled the people with awe.
No-one other than the High Priest dared to pronounce it.

To the ancient Hebrews, to know the name of something was
to know its essence, its character. In the Bible, when Moses asked
God to tell him His name, God's reply was deliberately evasive.
God's answer to Moses' question was: "I am that I am."[2] In his
reply, God was actually communicating this thought to Moses: To

know My name means that you truly know and understand who I am. But you cannot really know who I truly am. I shall show Myself to you only as I wish you to think of Me. What I truly am, however, will remain a mystery to you.

Perhaps even the Name pronounced by the High Priest was not God's true name!

In traditional Judaism, the mystery of God's name meant that what God really is must remain a mystery to man.

Therefore, to know God's holiest name and to meditate on it was, for Abraham Abulafia, the way to understand the mystery of who God really is.

The Journey of Abraham Abulafia

The life of Abraham Abulafia consisted of many journeys to discover many secrets. But in a sense, his life was one long journey to discover the secret of God's name.

Abraham ben Samuel Abulafia was born in Saragossa, Spain in the year 1240.[3] He spent his youth in Tudela, in the Spanish province of Navarre. He was taught Bible and Talmud by his father. When he was eighteen years old, his father died. Two years after his father's death, Abulafia journeyed to Israel. In Israel, he searched for remnants of the ten lost tribes who were, according to legend, living near the river Sambatyon. Abulafia traveled as far as Acre, on the coast of Israel. Moslem-Christian wars, however, interfered with his expedition. He left Israel, and spent the next ten years of his life in Greece and Italy.

During these ten years, Abulafia studied Moses Maimonides' *Guide of the Perplexed* under the tutelage of Hillel ben Samuel of Verona, a noted physician and scholar. Moses Maimonides was the greatest of the medieval Jewish philosophers. Born in Cordova, Spain in 1135, he spent most of his adult life in Egypt, dying there in 1204. Maimonides' most important philosophical book was the *Guide of the Perplexed*. The "perplexed" for whom it was intended were those who were unable to reconcile Jewish learning with the teachings of the Greek thinker Aristotle, whose philosophy dominated the Middle Ages. Maimonides' great achievement was to show that many of the beliefs of Judaism could be interpreted in a way that was compatible with Aristotle's teachings. Most remarkable of all, for Abulafia, was Maimonides' treatment of prophecy. Maimonides showed that it is possible for a person to train himself to become a prophet, by perfecting his intellect and his imagination. By so perfecting himself, an individual can become open to the influence of God. To Abulafia, this meant that prophecy was not confined to the past. After studying Maimonides' *Guide of the Perplexed*, Abulafia believed that he could become a prophet.

In 1270, Abulafia returned to Spain. Living in Barcelona, Abulafia began to study the *Kabbalah*. His study of *Kabbalah*, coupled with the influence of Maimonides, led to a remarkable experience. At the age of thirty-one, in Barcelona, Abulafia received his prophetic call. Abulafia believed he was overcome by the prophetic spirit. He believed that God was communicating with him, just as He communicated with prophets in the Bible such as Isaiah and Ezekiel. As a result of his "call," Abulafia believed that he obtained knowledge of the true name of God, and that he saw visions inspired by God.

After receiving his prophetic call, students came to study with Abulafia. He taught them about his prophecy and about his new method of meditation.

In 1274, Abulafia left Spain again and spent the rest of his life in Italy and Greece. In Italy, in 1280, he undertook a strange mission. He prepared to present himself before the Pope "in the name of the Jewish people." At this time, Abulafia probably believed that he was destined to be the Messiah. The notoriously anti-Semitic Pope Nicholas III had other plans. He planned to arrest Abulafia and have him burned at the stake. Fortunately for Abulafia, the Pope died before Abulafia came to see him. Abulafia was detained in the College of the Franciscans for twenty-eight days. He was then set free.

After this escape from death, Abulafia wandered about Italy for a number of years. Between the years 1279 and 1291, he wrote many books. Not all Jews reacted favorably to his claim of having received prophetic inspiration. He made many enemies among Jewish leaders. Nevertheless, despite his prophetic claims and his belief that he knew the great Name of God, Abulafia was actually a humble person. He truly believed in his mission, and required the highest standards of morality from his students. He taught his students a new method of meditation.

Abulafia's Way of Meditation

What was the purpose of Abulafia's meditation?

We are not able to know God through our five senses. Through our senses we see the physical world: mountains and lakes, deserts and oceans. When we look upward, we see the sun, the moon, the stars. This is what we can perceive with our five senses.

But Abulafia believed that what we perceive with our senses is not the only reality. If we had other senses, Abulafia thought, we would see the universe in an entirely different way. Abulafia believed that the ordinary world we see with our eyes is not the only world. Our world, he taught, is merely one among many worlds. Underlying all these worlds is the One Infinite Reality—God. The world we live in is only one of the ways in which God has manifested Himself.

Abulafia's way of meditation was designed to overcome the "sense barrier." Our senses, Abulafia taught, are barriers to the true knowledge of God. If we could go beyond our senses, Abulafia believed, we could know ourselves as part of the One; the Infinite Reality that is God.

The purpose of Abulafia's way of meditation, therefore, was to "break the sense barrier." In his own words, Abulafia said that his aim was "to unseal the soul, to untie the knots which bind it."[4] We are, according to Abulafia, "imprisoned" within our own bodies and apparently limited to what we can know through our five senses: what we can see, hear, touch, smell, and taste. These limitations Abulafia called "knots."

Science shows that what Abulafia said was true. We can only see a certain range of light waves. And we can only hear a certain range of sound waves.

But there is one way, Abulafia believed, in which we are not limited. In our power of thought, we can go beyond the senses. We can imagine other worlds besides our own. We can think about many things we cannot see.

Through meditation, Abulafia taught, we can reach a new state of consciousness. In this new level of consciousness, we can experience a higher spiritual reality: the power of God. To reach this higher level of consciousness, Abulafia needed an object upon which to meditate that would enable the mind to go beyond what can be perceived through the senses.

What object did Abulafia choose to meditate upon in order to stimulate the mind to reach a new state of consciousness?

The first stage of Abulafia's meditation focused on the letters of the Hebrew alphabet. He called his method *Hochmath Ha-Tseruf*—the science of the combination of letters.

Hebrew letters, to Abulafia, served as a spiritual language. He compared it to music. Just as musical notes are combined by a composer to make musical harmonies, so the combining of Hebrew letters stimulated a harmonious movement of pure thought in the mind of the meditator. Thinking about nothing but Hebrew letters and their possible combinations, the meditator was in a world of his own apart from the sense-world.

Abulafia's choice of the letters of the Hebrew alphabet, as objects to meditate on, had a basis in the Jewish tradition.[5] There is a legend that the Hebrew letters exist independently of ink and paper. The story is told of Rabbi Hananya ben Teradyon; he was wrapped in a scroll of the Torah and burned at the stake. Moments before his death, his students cried out: "Master! What do you see?" He answered: "The parchment is burning, but the letters are flying toward the heavens!"[6]

There is another legend that the letters of the Hebrew alphabet were mysteriously linked with God's creation of the world. The story is told of Bezalel, the architect of the tabernacle in the wilderness, that he knew how to combine the letters by which the world was created.[7]

These legends suggest the reasons for Abulafia's belief that meditation on Hebrew letters would lead to the knowledge of God.

Abulafia meditated on the Hebrew letters in three ways. He articulated their sounds. This was called *Mivta*—articulation. He wrote the letters. This stage was known as *Miktav*—writing. Finally, he thought about the letters. This was called *Mahshav*—thought.

By meditating on the Hebrew letters, the mind of the meditator was prepared for the highest stage—meditation on the holy Name of God.

We can imagine this final stage of meditation in this way:

> At the appointed hour, the Abulafian Kabbalist began permutating [combining] the letters of the *Tetragrammaton* (YHWH) with each of the five vowel sounds until he had accomplished every combination of the twelve possibilities given him by the master. . . . The best hour for *Tseruf* meditation was midnight, when, wrapped in prayer shawl and phylacteries, surrounded by many brilliantly lit candles, the Kabbalist started writing the sacred letters in black ink on white paper. Gathering speed as he permutated them, he felt a warm, glowing sensation at the heart, the sign of the descending *shefa* or divine influx. Singing certain names according to prescribed melodies, he attained ecstasy. . . . [8]

This was the goal of Abulafia's meditation: the feeling of God's overflowing power [influx] descending upon him. So moved was Abulafia himself by this meditation that he attained ecstasy.

What did Abulafia actually experience in his ecstasy?

Abulafia's Experience

As a result of his meditations on God's Name, Abraham Abulafia experienced a strange vision. He encountered his own self confronting and addressing him.

Here is a description of this experience:

> Know that the complete secret of prophecy consists for the prophet in that he suddenly sees the shape of his self standing before him and

he forgets his self and it is disengaged from him and he sees the shape
of his self before him talking to him and predicting the future.[9]

Ecstasy, we have seen, is the feeling of being outside one's body.
In Abulafia's prophetic ecstasy, the mystic sees his self standing in
front of him, addressing him.

Was this experience a vision of God?

Reflection

The way God appears to the mystic depends on the mystic's own
needs and experiences. God appears to different mystics in different ways. The vision of God which Abulafia saw was the vision
he needed to see. The secret of God's holy name—the God
Abulafia sought—was somehow connected with his own hidden
self.

Abulafia's vision teaches us that if we truly understand
ourselves, perhaps we can understand something about God.
Much of Jewish mysticism is actually a kind of commentary on the
verse in the Bible: "And God created man in His own image, in
the image of God created He him."[10]

The more we explore Jewish mysticism, the more we will see
the importance of understanding what man is, who we are.

6

The Scattered Sparks

During the first part of the Middle Ages, Spain was a great center of Jewish learning. It was in Spain, for example, that the *Zohar*, the classic book of Jewish mysticism, was written.

In the fifteenth century, the position of the Jews of Spain declined. Fanatical Church leaders forced the Jews to convert to Christianity. Many of those Jews who were forced to convert lived a Jewish life in secret. While professing to be Catholics in public, they tried to fulfill their obligations as Jews in private. The Church leaders hated these secret Jews and gave them the name "Marranos" or accursed.

The doom of Spanish Jewry was sealed when the Catholic sovereigns, Ferdinand and Isabella, issued a decree to appoint inquisitors in matters of faith on November 1, 1478. The inquisitorial court or *Inquisition* was directed against the Marranos. On February 6, 1481, the first *auto-da-fé* or "act of faith" was held: six men and six women were burned at the stake. The situation of the Jewish people rapidly deteriorated. Finally, on March 30, 1492, the dreaded decree went forth. By July 30, not a single Jew was allowed to remain in Spain. Any Jew who remained was to lose his life, unless he submitted to baptism. Approximately 150,000 Jews trudged toward the seaports to set forth for new homes![1]

After the expulsion from Spain in 1492, the Jewish population in Palestine grew considerably. For a great number of the incoming Spanish Jews, the city of Safed, situated on the loftiest hill of Galilee in the north, proved an attractive place to dwell. In the sixteenth century, Safed became a center where a new form of Jewish mysticism flourished.

The leader of the Jewish mystics of Safed was Rabbi Isaac Luria. Luria was called *"Ha-Ari,"* the "Ari" or the "Lion" of Safed. The name "Ha-Ari" was derived from the Hebrew initials of Ha-Elohi Rabbi Yitzhak[2]—The Divine Rabbi Isaac.

The new form of Jewish mysticism he initiated became known as the *Lurianic Kabbalah.* What was new about the mysticism he taught?

Before the expulsion from Spain, the focus of Jewish mysticism had been on *Maaseh Merkabah*—God's chariot and throne, and on *Maaseh Bereshis*—how the world was created. In contrast, the focus of Lurianic Kabbalah was the problem of suffering and evil, and how the world can be saved or redeemed.

Jews were troubled about the expulsion from Spain. They asked: "If God is good, why does He allow evil to occur? Why did God permit a tragedy like the expulsion from Spain to happen?"

This is a problem that is especially difficult for religious believers. If God is both all-powerful and all-good, He can prevent evil things from happening and he should not allow them to occur. How, then, can one believe that God really is all-powerful and all-good?

The Lurianic Kabbalists created an interesting theory in an attempt to solve this problem.

To understand their theory, it is important to know more about Isaac Luria and the other Jewish mystics of Safed.

The Ari (1534-1572).

Isaac Luria was born in Jerusalem in 1534. When he was only eight years of age, he was already considered a genius in the study of the Talmud. Shortly after his eighth birthday, his father died. His family then moved to the home of a wealthy uncle in Cairo, Egypt.

At the age of seventeen, Luria began to study *Kabbalah.* He first became acquainted with *Kabbalah* at a service he attended in a synagogue in Cairo. He saw a man at this service who was reading an unusual manuscript. Curious about this manuscript, Luria asked to see it. Fascinated by its contents, he purchased it from this visitor to the Cairo synagogue.

The manuscript that Luria purchased was the *Zohar*. Luria was so excited by the *Zohar* that he spent the next eight years of his life in intensive study of this book.

For this purpose, Luria went to live by himself in a small cottage on the banks of the Nile. While studying this book in solitude, he believed that the prophet Elijah appeared to him at night, in visions, to initiate him into the study of the secrets of the *Zohar*.[3]

After another eight years of solitary study, the Ari believed that Elijah appeared to him and advised him to move from Cairo to Safed. Elijah also told him that he was not to live very much longer, and that his final mission in life awaited him in Safed.

In the year 1569, Isaac Luria arrived at Safed. There he gathered a group of disciples around him. The period of his activity in Safed was brief; he died on July 15, 1572. His grave became a place of pilgrimage for future generations. Other great men also played a part in the development of Jewish mysticism in Safed.

Joseph Caro (1488-1575).

Joseph Caro was a great Jewish legalist as well as a Kabbalist. He was born in Spain in the year 1488. He was forced to leave Spain with his father in 1492. After many wanderings and great suffering, they settled in Turkey. There he began his work on Jewish law.

Joseph Caro's major work in Jewish law was his book *Beit Joseph*—the "House of Joseph". This book was a commentary on Rabbi Jacob ben Asher's "Digest of the Law", the *Arba Turim* or "Four Rows". In this book, Caro traced each law to its original source.[4] It was one of the most important works ever written on Jewish law. Caro spent thirty years of his life (1522-1552) writing this book.

Caro wrote another book on Jewish law, however, which became more popular than the *Beit Joseph*. In the aftermath of the tragedy of the expulsion from Spain in 1492, (which spread the idea that Jews ought not to live in Christian society) the condition of European Jewry in the sixteenth century worsened. What was needed was a code of Jewish law, which would bring structure and order to the variety of local customs. Caro wrote such a code to answer this need; the *Shulchan Aruch* or "Prepared Table". This work became the standard code of Jewish law; Orthodox Jews today still live according to the rules of the *Shulchan Aruch*.

Joseph Caro, however, was not only a legalist. In addition to his great contribution to *Halacha* (Jewish law), Caro also wrote an important Kabbalistic book. The name of this book was the *Maggid Mesharim*. It was a mystical diary describing what Caro believed were nightly meetings with an angel, called the *Maggid*. This angel, Caro said, acted as an instructor (*Maggid*) to him—telling him what actions to perform, and what not to do. The angel instructed him to be humble, not to become angry, to be conscious of his sins and to say his prayers with devotion. But the angel not only gave him instructions. Caro was also offered a great deal of love and affection by the angel. The *Maggid* or *Mentor-Angel* of Joseph Caro was actually a kind of parent to him.

In 1536, Joseph Caro left Turkey for Safed. There he headed a *Bet Din* and was regarded as the leading scholar in Safed. One of Caro's pupils was Moses Cordovero, who, with Solomon Alkabetz, established the custom of *Tikkun Leil Shavuos*—staying awake on Shavuos eve to study Torah.

Solomon Alkabetz (ca. 1505-1584)

Very little is known about the life of Solomon Alkabetz. He used to go regularly with his students to the graves of dead saints, it is said, where they believed that they could commune with the souls of the departed. They lived according to strict rules of piety and goodness. They judged themselves very severely if they fell short of these high standards. To utter a profane word, for example, was considered by them to be a grievous sin.

The high point of the week was the Sabbath. On Sabbath eve, he and his students went into the streets of Safed to welcome the

Sabbath Queen. Solomon Alkabetz is best known for his poem, *Lechah Dodi*, "Come, my Beloved", which he wrote to express his love and the love of his comrades for the Sabbath. The Sabbath was personified as a queen, or bride. The comrades loved the Sabbath as a king loves his queen, as a groom loves his bride.

Alkabetz's poem, *Lechah Dodi*, became one of the highlights of the standard *Kabalat Shabat* service—the Sabbath-eve service welcoming the Sabbath. The six Psalms preceding the *Lechah Dodi* in the Sabbath-eve service were selected by Alkabetz's best-known disciple and brother-in-law, Moses Cordovero.

Moses Cordovero (1522-1570)

Moses Cordovero was born in 1522. Although his birthplace is unknown, the name "Cordovero" indicates his family's Spanish origins.

Cordovero acted as one of the *Dayanim* (judges) of Safed,[5] and was a disciple of Alkabetz and Caro.

Of all the Kabbalists of Safed in the Sixteenth century, Cordovero possessed the most brilliant theoretical mind. His major book, *Pardes* (the Garden), gave order and system to the *Kabbalah*.

The relationship between Isaac Luria and Moses Cordovero was an interesting one. Luria was the inspired leader, Cordovero the thinker. Luria wrote very little, Cordovero wrote many books. In fact, we would know very little about Isaac Luria's Kabbalistic theory if his chief disciple, Hayyim Vital (1543-1620) had not kept an accurate record of Luria's lectures and discussions.

Isaac Luria himself was a disciple of Moses Cordovero. The genius of Moses Cordovero was an inspriation to Isaac Luria. But Isaac Luria brought Cordovero's thoughts to life.

Isaac Luria's Question

Safed reached its zenith in 1569 with the arrival of Isaac Luria. Hayyim Vital, a scholarly Rabbi living in Damascus, suddenly saw visions of a great leader arising in Safed. Vital journeyed to Safed and found his vision to be proven correct.[6] Isaac Luria was quickly recognized as a charismatic personality. And Hayyim Vital became Luria's chief disciple.

Picture a saintly, mysterious man walking with his disciples through the hills of Safed. As they walk together, Luria teaches the wisdom and knowledge of his new theory.

Imagine that you are one of Luria's disciples, one of his students. After walking through the hills of Safed, Luria invites you and his other students to sit down under a tree. As you look up at the mountains and the sky in the lovely setting of Safed, the master—the Ari—begins his lesson by asking a question.

"If God is everywhere," Luria asks, "how can there be space enough for the world to exist?"

If you were one of Luria's students, you would be puzzled by this question. You have been taught that "God is everywhere." But surely you never thought of God as actually occupying all of space. Is this what Isaac Luria really meant?

Isaac Luria took very seriously the idea that God is everywhere. Although Luria did not believe that God occupies space in the same way that something physical—such as a spaceship—takes up space, he did believe that God was the most powerful force in existence. It was his belief in God's omnipresence that led Isaac Luria to ask this question. Luria believed that God was such a powerful force that no person or thing could co-exist with Him in the world.

According to Luria's idea, then, how could the world have been created? There were three parts to Luria's theory. The first was called *Tzimtzum*.

Tzimtzum

The Hebrew word *Tzimtzum* means withdrawal or retreat. The idea of *Tzimtzum* is illustrated by the following story:

> When a father sets out to teach his little son to walk, he stands in front of him and holds his two hands on either side of the child so that he cannot fall, and the boy goes toward his father between his father's hands. But the moment he is close, his father moves away a little

and holds his hands further apart. The father does this over and over so that the child may learn to walk.[7]

Just as a parent must eventually withdraw to allow a child to develop the freedom to walk on his own, so, Isaac Luria believed, God must withdraw to allow the world to develop according to its own natural laws, and to allow man the freedom and growth to choose between good and evil. God withdraws to allow man to develop his own freedom and autonomy.

According to Isaac Luria, God withdrew in order for the world itself to exist. Luria called this act of God's withdrawal *Tzimtzum*. By this act of *Tzimtzum*, God makes room for our world by retreating from a portion of His universe.

By retreating, God gave man the freedom to exist on his own and to choose between good and evil, as an independent individual, responsible for his own choice.

Why did God create a world in which evil was even a possibility? Why didn't God create a world that was perfectly good?

The next two parts of Isaac Luria's theory were attempts to answer these questions.

The "Breaking of the Vessels"

Isaac Luria used symbols and myths to explain his theory. A symbol, we learned, is a visible sign of something intangible. For example, in the sentence: "A lion is a symbol of courage," the "lion" is a visible representation of an invisible, intangible value—courage.

The word "myth" is often misunderstood. People think a myth is merely a fairy tale. A myth is really much more. It is a story that is told in answer to questions such as: 'What happened at the beginning of time?' 'Why is there evil in the world?' The story of Adam and Eve in the Bible is a myth. There are Greek myths that tell the stories of the gods on Mount Olympus. There are myths in every culture.

The story that Isaac Luria told was a myth which tried to explain why God had allowed the terrible suffering and tragedy of the exile from Spain to occur in 1492. Luria's myth was called "the breaking of the vessels." According to this myth, there is a flaw in our world. The reason for this flaw lies in what happened after God withdrew to allow the creation of the world.

According to a legend, God created and destroyed many worlds before He created our world.[8] Isaac Luria's myth gave greater meaning to this legend.[9]

Luria's myth starts with the symbol of light. Light is a symbol of God. Just as a person can be blinded by too much exposure to the sun, so were these first worlds destroyed because the light that first came forth from God was too strong, too powerful.

These first worlds which God created after His retreat were called "vessels."[10] The destruction of these worlds was called "the breaking of the vessels."[11] This cosmic catastrophe preceded the creation of our world.

Because of this accident, our world is imperfect; broken fragments of these vessels fell down into our world. These broken fragments—called *Kelippot* (shells or husks)—are a symbol of evil.[12] Evil, to Isaac Luria, was a real force. It was called "the other side": the realm of the devil, the realm of destruction. Evil, to Luria, was not merely the absence of good. Evil forces really existed.

Why did Luria consider these broken fragments the symbol of evil? Evil destroys; evil shatters; evil breaks the order of the world. Because the order of the world was broken, nothing in this world is in its proper place; everything is like broken fragments.[13]

Now, "exile" is precisely the state of being removed from one's rightful place. The Jews of his time were crushed by the exile from Spain; Luria helped them and taught them through this myth that nothing in the whole world was in its proper place. He saw that the evil rulers of Spain were triumphant, the Jews were exiled. He saw that the wicked seemed to have better lives than the good. The whole world, therefore, seemed to Isaac Luria to be a mistake, a flaw. The world as it was was not the world as it ought to be.

Did Isaac Luria see any hope in this situation?

Tikkun

Isaac Luria believed that God intended the world to be good. He believed that for the world to be good, man had to have freedom of choice. And for man to be free to choose, there had to be the possibility of evil. This is the reason why God allowed the "breaking of the vessels" to occur.

God also gave man the power to combat evil. How did God help man to fight the forces of evil?

Light, we remember, is a symbol of God. Fire manifests light. Sparks are part of fire. Sparks are thus a symbol of the presence of God.

Isaac Luria believed that sparks of God's presence existed in the world. The scattered sparks of God's light, Luria said, were imprisoned in the *Kelippot*—the broken fragments of the vessels. It is the task of the Jew, according to Luria, to free these scattered sparks from the shells in which they are imprisoned; to raise them up and re-unite them with God.[14]

This myth gave purpose to the suffering of Jews in exile. The purpose of the Jews' exile was to extract the last sparks of goodness or Godliness scattered among the nations; to find the good and the holy within the world.[15]

By searching for the good, Luria believed, man can repair or mend the flaws in the world. Man can restore the world to its original harmony, the way it was before the impact of the *Kelippot* on the earth.

This process of mending the world, of correcting its mistakes, Luria called *Tikkun.*

It is a traditional Jewish belief that man and God are partners in the betterment of the world. Isaac Luria elaborated upon this concept, placing the major emphasis upon man.

Luria believed that man plays a role in the redemption, in the salvation of the world. The Jew, in particular, helps to save the world by seeking the good, by performing *Mitzvot.* The religious acts of the Jew help to redeem the world.

How will man know that the world has in fact been redeemed?

How will man know that *Tikkun*—the mending of the world—has taken place?

The sign that *Tikkun* has taken place will be the coming of the Messiah.

Lurianic Kabbalah, with its belief in *Tikkun*, stimulated a hope for the coming of the Messiah. In the seventeenth century, the fulfillment of Luria's hope seemed to come true in the person of Sabbatai Zevi, a man whom many Jews believed was the long awaited Messiah.

What did Jewish mystics believe about the perfected man, the ideal leader? Who was Sabbatai Zevi? Why did so many Jews believe he was the Messiah?

These are some of the questions we shall discuss in Part III.

Reflection

Isaac Luria preferred a world where man was free to choose, even if this meant the possibility of evil. A perfect world where man was merely a puppet of God was not his ideal.

Issac Luria's theory, therefore, makes us think about this question: What is more important—freedom or perfection?

The way we think about this question depends upon which of these two values is more important to us. The answer we give to this question tells us something about what we think man is, and what he is capable of becoming.

It is to a study of Jewish mystical ideas about *man*—about what man is, and about who the ideal man is—that we now turn.

Part Three

MAN

7

What Is Man?

What is man?* How does man differ from other living things? The way we think about man depends on our point of view.

To a biologist, man is a highly complex animal, an intricate organism.

To a philosopher, man is an animal who thinks, an animal with a mind: a rational animal.

To a psychologist, man is an emotional animal: an animal who loves, hates, fears, and hopes.

The Kabbalist sees man in a different way. A modern Jewish mystic need not deny Darwin's theory of evolution.[1] But he would nevertheless insist that there is something about man that makes him entirely different from an animal.

This special quality of man is his "soul," the "image of God" in him.

In the Jewish tradition, man has always been regarded as precious and special to God. But it is in the Jewish mystical tradition—the *Kabbalah*—that the uniqueness of man, his "soul," is most eloquently expressed.

How is "man" described in the Jewish tradition? What does the *Kabbalah* add to the Jewish concept of man? And what does the Kabbalistic idea of man teach us about ourselves?

"Man" in the Bible
Judaism teaches the essential value and importance of every

---

*We are using the term "man" in the sense of "human being": to indicate both male and female.

human being. This idea of the worth of the individual is expressed
in the story of Creation in the Bible:

> And God said, "Let us make man in our own image, after our like-
> ness; and let them have dominion over the fish of the sea, and over the
> fowl of the air, and over the cattle, and over all the earth, and over
> every creeping thing that creepeth upon the earth." And God created
> man in His own image, in the image of God created He him; male and
> female created He them.[2]

The Torah here assumes that the appearance of man upon the
earth was not an accident. On the contrary! Man was the result of
God's deliberation.

The Torah further assumes that within every individual—both
male and female—there is some element that resembles God, the
Creator. What is this element in man that is in "the image of
God", and that sets him apart from the animal kingdom?

This new aspect of man is set forth as the story of Creation
continues:

> Then the Lord God formed man of the dust of the ground, and
> breathed into his nostrils the breath of life; and man became a living
> soul.[3]

The image of God in man is the "living soul." It is the soul that
makes us different from the rest of the animal kingdom. We have
already learned that the soul is that part of man which is immortal—that lives on after death. It is also the soul which understands
our relationship to God, that we are created in His image.[4] It is
the soul within us that provides the still, small voice of conscience,
urging us to obey the Torah—the will of God:

> All creatures that are formed of heaven, both their soul and body are
> heavenly; and all creatures that are formed of earth, both their soul
> and body are earthbound, with the exception of mankind, whose soul
> is from heaven and his body is from earth.
> Therefore, if a man obeys the Torah and does the will of his Father

in heaven, behold he is like the creatures above; as it is written: "I have said, You are gods, and all of you sons of the Most High."

But if he obey not the Torah and perform not the will of his Father in heaven, he is like the creatures below; as it is said: "Nevertheless, you shall die like men."[5]

The first man, Adam, was given an opportunity to be like the angels—the heavenly creatures. He was placed by God in the Garden of Eden—the Heavenly Paradise.

But one thing was prohibited to him. He was commanded by God not to eat of the fruit of the "tree of the knowledge of good and evil" in the midst of the garden.

Adam disobeyed this one commandment, and disappointed God. After eating the forbidden fruit, Adam heard the voice of God, asking him: "Where art Thou?"

Surely, God knew where Adam was. God was not seeking information. God was rather seeking to reach Adam's conscience.

Adam replied to God that he had "hidden himself." But can man really hide from God?

A Hasidic teacher commented on this Biblical story:

> Adam hides himself to avoid rendering accounts, to escape responsibility for his way of living. Every man hides for this purpose, for every man is Adam and finds himself in Adam's situation. . . . The situation can be precisely defined as follows: Man cannot escape the eye of God, but in trying to hide from him, he is hiding from himself.[6]

Adam represents all men, every individual. Adam was given the choice between good and evil. So, too, is every person. Adam tried to hide from God. So, too, do all men.

Adam forfeited the opportunity to remain in Paradise. God drove him out of the Garden of Eden. So, too, there is a destructive tendency in man—his *Yetzer Ha-Ra* or evil impulse[7]—that ruins many paradises for him.

But Adam possessed a soul—a soul that made him "little lower than the angels." So, too, deep within every individual is a soul—the still small voice of conscience. In the Bible, Adam, as the symbol of man, represents dignity. In the *Kabbalah*, we shall learn that Adam, symbol of man, represents dignity, and many other qualities, too.

It is this dignity of every human being that is the major theme of the concept of man in the Bible. One of its finest expressions is in Psalm 8, when the Psalmist speaks these words to God:

> When I behold Your heavens, the work of Your fingers, the moon and the stars, which You have established; What is man, that You are mindful of him? And the son of man, that You think of him?
>
> Yet You have made man but little lower than the angels, and have crowned him with glory and honor. You have caused him to rule over the works of Your hands; You have put all things beneath his feet.[8]

"Man" in the Talmud

In the Talmud, man is compared to a world:

> Man was first created as a single individual (Adam) to teach the lesson that whoever destroys one life, Scripture ascribes it to him as though he had destroyed a whole world; and whoever saves one life, Scripture ascribes it to him as though he had saved a whole world.[9]

The Talmud here powerfully communicates the concept of the supreme value of every individual life. This is an idea that many people living in the twentieth century have forgotten.

In the twentieth century, we think in terms of statistics. For example, we refer to the "six million" Jews, who perished during the Holocaust in the concentration camps of Nazi Germany. By referring to the "six million", we think in terms of an abstraction. How much more cogently is the tragedy of the Holocaust conveyed, if we look at it in terms of one little boy cast into a crematorium fire to be burned to death!

Modern man has much to learn from the Talmud, and its assertion that every individual is as important as an entire world.

"Man" in the Kabbalah

Of all aspects of the Jewish tradition, the *Kabbalah*, the Jewish

mystical tradition, gave the highest place to man. In the *Zohar,*
man is the crown of creation. He is called *Shechinta Tataa*—the
"miniature" presence of God on earth. Man has a choice: either
to make God's presence alive on earth by his good deeds, or to
deny God's presence, the spark of the Divine within him.

In the Lurianic Kabbalah, man is given an even higher place in
God's world. The first being to issue forth from God, according to
Isaac Luria, was *Adam Kadmon. Adam Kadmon* means "the
original man." God can be compared to an architect. Before an architect builds an actual house, he first creates a model, a plan, a
blueprint for the house. So, too, the Lurianic Kabbalists believed,
before God created man on earth, He created a model in heaven
from which to pattern him. *Adam Kadmon* was the name given to
"heavenly" man. Luria believed that *Adam Kadmon* was the pattern for all creation. This was a symbol of the great importance of
man in God's plan for the world.

Adam on earth, Luria thus taught, was made in the image of
Adam Kadmon—the heavenly man. Every limb of Adam's body
was a reflection of each limb of *Adam Kadmon.*[10] Just as *Adam
Kadmon*—Heavenly man—was given dominion over the heavenly
spheres, so earthly man was commanded to rule over the animal
kingdom.

Because of his likeness to *Adam Kadmon*, Adam was given an
important task. Adam was given the opportunity to mend the
world, after the tragedy of the "breaking of the vessels." Adam
had the power of *Tikkun*—to restore the original harmony of the
world. Furthermore, Luria said that all human souls, the Divine
spark of all individuals ever to be born, existed potentially in
Adam.

We can understand this idea if we realize that "Adam," the
name of the first man on earth, is also the Hebrew word for man.
All human beings, Judaism teaches, are descendants of Adam.
Since all human beings have the same ancestor, no human being
can claim to be superior to any other.[11] And what man is today, so
Luria taught, is a consequence of what Adam did.

In Luria's myth, the fate of the whole world rested on whether

Adam would be successful in *Tikkun*—in mending the world. Everything depended on Adam's choice: to obey or to disobey the commandment of God.

Luria's myth thus stressed the importance of each individual's choice. We are always confronted with the necessity of making decisions. Quite often, such a decision involves a choice between good and evil. Isaac Luria believed that a world where man was free to choose—even if it meant the possibility of choosing evil—was better than a perfect world in which man was not given the freedom to choose. This idea was also found in the *Zohar*:

> Before creating the world, God created many others without the Torah. Because He had created them, each of these worlds was perfect, each of them beautiful—but, they were meaningless worlds because they were static and did not grow or change. In these previous worlds, there was no lust, but there was no love, either. There was perfect satisfaction, but there was no ambition. There was no strife, but no peace. There was no sorrow, but no joy, either. Everything was without flaw, but there was no hope of anything becoming better.
>
> The real spark of life—freedom, free will, the chance and the ability to choose good from evil, to sin with a chance to repent, the ability to create or to fail—these were missing.
>
> The world, which God created using the Torah as His plan, is a dynamic world, a world in which man can choose.[12]

Like the author of this passage in the *Zohar*, Isaac Luria believed that a world in which man was free—even though evil was a real possibility—was better than a perfect world. Therefore, Adam was given freedom to choose.

But, alas, Adam failed. Adam sinned: he disobeyed God's commandment. His sin had far-reaching consequences. Adam's opportunity for *Tikkun* was lost. And Adam's failure made the task of all future men much more difficult, but that much more important.

To the Kabbalists, therefore, man's role in the world is a very important one. They believed that what man does has an effect upon the world and upon God. They believed that man was not only a partner with God but also that God needed man for *Tik-kun*—for the mending of His world.

Here, then, is the Kabbalistic concept of man in relation to God. It is the idea that "man's relationship to God should not be that of passive reliance"[13] upon His power. Rather it should be a relationship of "active assistance."[14] God needs man's help to mend His imperfect world. Man was placed on this earth for *Tikkun*—to correct what is wrong, and to improve and perfect God's world.

Thus, of all the Jewish sages, the Kabbalists placed the most stress on the potential greatness of man. Everything that man does on earth, they believed, has an effect on heaven. The first earthly man, Adam, was patterned after the heavenly man, *Adam Kadmon.*

And we ourselves are reflections of the original soul of the first man—Adam. Where Adam failed, our task is to succeed in *Tikkun:* the mending of God's world. By creating peace here on earth, the Kabbalist says, we bring peace to the Most High—God.

Reflection

The Kabbalists placed great emphasis upon man. Perhaps they exaggerated man's power in the universe. Nevertheless, the point they wished to make about "man" is important and relevant to us in the twentieth century.

To be sure, our concept of the universe today is different from that of Isaac Luria in the seventeenth century. Man was clearly the center of Isaac Luria's universe. Today, however, we know that the earth, man's dwelling place, is an infinitesimal part of a vast universe. Considered in the light of the immensity of the universe as we know it today, man seems insignificant.

Yet, today, as never before, we need to think about the value of each individual, the worth of man. The Kabbalistic concepts of the preciousness of man to God and the potential greatness of the individual, added to the Biblical and Talmudic idea of the dignity of man, offer an important teaching to our world today.

Contrast what the Kabbalists taught about man with the following definition of man often quoted in pre-Nazi Germany:

> The human body contains a sufficient amount of fat to make seven cakes of soap, enough iron to make a medium-sized nail, a sufficient amount of phosphorus to equip two thousand match-heads, enough sulphur to rid one's self of one's fleas.[15]

Surely there was a connection between this view of man and what the Nazis did in the concentration camps: make soap of human flesh.

Our world needs to know the Kabbalistic concept of the greatness of man. We need to be reminded once again that man is "little lower than the angels" and that every individual is unique because his soul is precious to God.

8

The Mystical Messiah

Ideas often exert a powerful effect upon history. The main idea of
the new *Kabbalah* of Isaac Luria was the concept of *Tikkun*. The
concept of *Tikkun*, as we learned, meant that man's task was to
mend a broken world, to perfect the world.

The lives of many Jews in the sixteenth century were indeed
broken lives. A multitude of Jews had been exiled from Spain in
1492. Spain had not been the only country to expel the Jews. In
1290, the Jews had been expelled from England; and in 1394 the
Jews had been driven out of France. At the close of the Middle
Ages, many Jews were thus left with insecurity of residence and
stunted, broken lives.

Why, the Jews asked, did God allow such tragedies to occur?
How could their tragic plight be reconciled with the concept of
the Jews as the "chosen people" of God? Why, if they were
chosen, were they persecuted and exiled?

Isaac Luria had tried to explain the meaning of their suffering to
the Jewish people of his time. The Jews, he believed, were dispersed among the nations of the world to discover and to lift up
the traces or sparks of God's presence among the Gentiles. No
matter how evil a person seemed to be, no matter how wicked a
nation appeared, there were Divine sparks hidden there. As Luria
symbolically expressed it, the Divine sparks were enclosed within
evil shells or husks (the *Kelippot*). This meant that even if someone
seemed evil on the outside, if you looked deeply enough inside,
you would find evidence of God's presence.

The Jew's task, in particular, was to make man aware of these traces or sparks of God. In this way, man could repair a broken and confused world: by correcting abuses and injustice, by righting wrongs and by transforming evil into good. *Tikkun*—improving the world, mending its flaws—was the watchword of Isaac Luria.

These ideas of Isaac Luria did not remain mere theories. Luria's ideas, coupled with a strange course of events, led to the rise of a Jewish mystical Messiah: Sabbatai Zevi.

What did Jews believe about the Messiah? How did the idea of a mystical Messiah differ from the traditional Jewish concept of the Messiah? Who was Sabbatai Zevi? And why did so many Jews come to believe that he was the Messiah?

The Concept of the Messiah

The word "Messiah" comes from the Hebrew word *Mashiah*. *Mashiah* means "anointed with oil." In the Bible, kings and high priests are described by this word, because they were anointed with oil. Anointing with oil was a means of coronation. It was a symbol of selection for a special, important purpose.[1]

The word *Mashiah* thus became a title of honor signifying "the chosen one." During the days of the First Temple, when the Jews in Israel were troubled by problems and pressures from neighboring states, the prophet Isaiah expressed the hope for a king who would be so wise and just that his reign would bring political peace. This concept of the ideal king and leader came to be designated by the term *Mashiah* or Messiah.

The Messiah, originally, was thus an ordinary human being who was "special" because he was a great political leader. He was not considered to be a supernatural being—above or unrelated to other human beings. He was to be a descendant of King David, who had been promised that the throne would remain in his family forever.

As time passed, however, the concept of the Messiah did take on supernatural aspects. During the sixth century, a prophet who has come to be known as Second Isaiah, gave hope to the exiled Jews in Babylonia after the destruction of the First Temple in 586 B.C.E. He considered the Jewish people as a group to be the

Messiah, the "suffering servant of the Lord." The Jewish people, Second Isaiah believed, suffered to atone for the sins of the other nations of the world. Through Israel's suffering, this prophet believed, the whole world would be saved.

Second Isaiah depicted the Jewish people as if they were a single individual. Here is a portion of Second Isaiah's description of the "suffering servant of the Lord":

> *He was despised, and forsaken of men,*
> *A man of pains, and acquainted with disease,*
> *And as one from whom men hide their face:*
> *He was despised, and we esteemed him not.*
> *Surely our diseases he did bear, and our pains he carried;*
> *Whereas we did esteem him stricken,*
> *Smitten of God, and afflicted.*
> *But he was wounded because of our transgressions,*
> *He was crushed because of our iniquities.* [2]

Christians interpreted this passage from Isaiah as a reference to their Messiah and savior—Jesus Christ. "Christ" comes from the Greek word *Christos*, and is the Greek equivalent of the Hebrew word *Mashiah*. To the Christian, Jesus was a supernatural Messiah—the son of God—whose death by crucifixion atoned for the sins of mankind.

Jewish Biblical scholars, however, believe that Second Isaiah personified the Jewish people as an individual suffering servant of the Lord. They do not think that Second Isaiah was predicting the advent of the Christian Messiah.

The Jewish people as a group, did not believe that Jesus was the Messiah. Most of the Jews felt that he was guilty of blasphemy, when he referred to himself as the son of God. Moreover, his coming did not bring peace—which was associated with the coming of the Messiah.

Furthermore, the Jewish people had always been cautioned against false prophets and false Messiahs. For example, there was a saying in Talmudic times: "If you are engaged in planting, and someone says that the Messiah is coming, finish what you are doing."[3] Jews thus had always been taught to be patient and cautious—not to impulsively follow someone who rises up and claims to be the Messiah.

Yet, in the seventeenth century, the majority of the Jewish people were swept up by the Messianic claims of Sabbatai Zevi. How could the Jewish people—with their tradition of reasonableness, caution and patience—become convinced that this one very strange man, Sabbatai Zevi, was the Messiah? Who was this man who so captured the minds and hearts of the Jews?

Who was Sabbatai Zevi?

Sabbatai Zevi was born in Smyrna, Turkey on the ninth day of the Hebrew month Av in 1626. The Ninth of Av—the day commemorating the destruction of the First and Second Temples—fell on a Sabbath in the year 1626. Jewish children who were born on the Sabbath were frequently called Sabbatai during this period of history.

Sabbatai's day of birth was auspicious. There was an ancient Rabbinic tradition that the date of the destruction of the Second Temple was to be the date of birth of the Messiah. The evidence indicates that Sabbatai definitely was born on the ninth of Av, for the ninth of Av in the year 1626 (corresponding to the Hebrew year 5386) did fall on a Sabbath. His date of birth was, therefore, not contrived to fit his Messianic claims.[4]

Sabbatai came from a wealthy family. His father, Mordecai, acted as a broker for an English mercantile firm. In the Christian circles in which his father traveled, it was believed that the year 1666 was the year of redemption, when Jews would be restored to Palestine. Surely Sabbatai's father communicated this to his son. But among Jewish Kabbalists, the year 1648 was prophesied as the date of the Messianic redemption. The superstitious character of the age is seen in these speculations about the year of salvation.

As a young man, Sabbatai received thorough religious training in the study of the Talmud in the Rabbinical school of Joseph Escapa.

During his adolescent years, he began to devote himself to the study of *Kabbalah,* delving into the *Zohar* and other mystical works. His study of the *Kabbalah* coincided with the beginning of his bizarre behavior and strange acts. He took frequent ritual baths of purification in the sea—at night as well as by day, in winter as well as in summer. He married and divorced twice in the space of a few years. And he was subject to frequent changes of mood.

As Sabbatai Zevi approached his twentieth year, his changes of mood began to indicate the presence of emotional illness. The normal person, to be sure, experiences changes of mood: some days he feels "up," at other times he feels "down." But in the case of a normal person, such mood swings are not self-destructive.

In the case of Sabbatai Zevi, however, the "up" swings were states of excessive exaltation to the point of ecstasy. The "downs" were periods of utter depression and dejection, agony and anguish. It became clear that Sabbatai Zevi definitely suffered from an emotional illness. This illness was characterized by the extreme "ups" and "downs" Sabbatai experienced. But what was unique about his emotional illness was that it left his mind intact. And the fact that he suffered from an emotional illness did not work against his eventual messianic claims. On the contrary! The Messiah, as depicted by Second Isaiah, was to be "a man of pains, and acquainted with disease."

Furthermore, Sabbatai Zevi was tall of stature and impressive in appearance. He also possessed a pleasing voice and sang beautifully. No wonder, then, that by the age of twenty he had attracted a group of disciples, whom he instructed in the mysteries of Kabbalah.

The year 1648 was a crucial year in the history of the Jewish people and a decisive year in the history of *Kabbalah.*

The year of 1648, as we learned, was deemed to be in some Kabbalistic circles the year of the coming of the Messiah. According to the traditional Jewish concept, the coming of the Messiah was to be preceded by "Hevlei Ha-Mashiah"—the "birth-pangs" of the Messiah: severe catastrophe and agony were to precede the advent of the Messiah.

In 1648, a severe catastrophe did happen to the Jewish people.

It was in 1648 that Jewish communities in the Ukraine and in Poland were massacred by Cossack hordes, under the leadership of Bogdan Chmielnitzki. Victims were flayed and burned alive. Women and infants were mutilated and slaughtered. Thousands of Jews perished. Only those who were willing to embrace the Greek Orthodox faith of the Cossacks—a Christian group who lived east of the Dnieper—survived.

It was also in 1648 that Sabbatai Zevi gave the first indication of his claim to be the Messiah. He began to pronounce God's holy name—the *Tetragrammaton*—in public. This was an act of great daring, and a momentous break with the centuries-old Jewish tradition of not pronouncing God's name the way it is actually written in the Bible.

Sabbatai Zevi's daring act did not go unchallenged. Joseph Escapa—the head of the Rabbinical school—and his colleagues excommunicated Sabbatai Zevi. But there were other members of the community, such as the influential Moses Pinheiro, who truly believed that Sabbatai was the Messiah. They accepted Sabbatai's excommunication as part of the persecutions expected in the career of the Messiah.

Driven out of Smyrna, Sabbatai proceeded to Salonika, which by then had the largest Jewish population in the Turkish Empire. There he performed one of the most striking of his *Maasim Zarim*—his strange actions. He invited the most prominent Rabbis of Salonika to a banquet. At the banquet, he erected a bridal canopy, had a Torah scroll brought in, and performed a marriage ceremony between himself and the Torah. This strange ceremony represented, to Sabbatai Zevi, the mystical union of himself as the Messiah, with the Torah, conceived of as the heavenly daughter. Outraged by this seemingly sacrilegious act of Sabbatai Zevi, the Rabbis banished him from Salonika. After leaving Salonika, Sabbatai wandered from country to country without friends or real followers. Perhaps he began to have doubts about his Messianic mission.

The turning point in his life occurred when he settled in Jerusalem in 1662. For in Jerusalem, Sabbatai attracted the attention of the man who was to become his staunchest supporter, and who was to make the Jewish world aware of his Messianic mission. This man was Nathan of Gaza (1644-1680).

Nathan's full name was Abraham Nathan ben Elisha Hayyim Ashkenazi. As a young man, Nathan was a brilliant student of the Talmud. He possessed a powerful mind. In 1664, Nathan took up the study of *Kabbalah*. He delved deeply into *Lurianic Kabbalah*. He not only studied Luria's teachings; he fasted, he prayed, and he meditated in his thirst for mystical experience. After a short time, he began to have visions of angels and deceased souls. This was only the beginning of Nathan's mystical experiences.

At that time, Nathan heard a great deal about the strange personality and the trials and tribulations of Sabbatai Zevi. He saw him many times in Jerusalem and was impressed by Sabbatai's appearance and presence. Nathan's impression of Sabbatai Zevi went beyond appearances, however. Nathan became convinced that Sabbatai Zevi was the Messiah. This conviction was confirmed to Nathan in a vision he experienced, and described in a letter written in 1667:

> In that same year, my force having been stimulated by the visions of the angels and the blessed souls, I was undergoing a long fast in the week after the feast of Purim. Having now locked myself in holiness and purity in a separate room and completed the morning prayer under many tears, the spirit came over me, my hair stood on end and my knees shook and I saw the *Merkabah*, and I saw visions of God all day long and all night, and I was vouchsafed true prophecy like any other prophet, as the voice spoke to me and began with the words: "Thus speaks the Lord." And with the utmost clarity my heart perceived towards whom my prophecy was directed [toward Sabbatai Zevi], and until this day I have never yet had so great a vision, but it remained hidden in my heart until the Redeemer revealed himself in Gaza and proclaimed himself the Messiah; only then did the angel permit me to proclaim what I had seen.[5]

As a result of visions such as this, Nathan of Gaza acquired a reputation as a wise man and as a healer of souls. Now, Sabbatai

Zevi, we already know, suffered from an emotional illness. Having heard of the remarkable healing powers of Nathan, Sabbatai went to Gaza, in Israel, to find "peace for his soul." Here we confront one of the most incredible ironies in Jewish history. Sabbatai Zevi went to see Nathan of Gaza, as a patient to a doctor—hoping that Nathan could cure him of his emotional illness. But Nathan had a different idea of this meeting. When they met, Nathan convinced Sabbatai Zevi that he truly was the Messiah. Thus, it was the meeting of these two men that led to Sabbatai's proclamation of himself as the Messiah in Gaza in 1665.

The "Messiahship" of Sabbatai Zevi thus became a movement—the Sabbatian movement. Nathan of Gaza was a brilliant organizer and spokesman for Sabbatai Zevi. The widespread effect the Sabbatian movement began to have was largely due to Nathan of Gaza.

The Sabbatian Movement

In the fall of 1665, Sabbatai Zevi returned to Smyrna. In the synagogue in Smyrna, he publicly proclaimed himself as the Messiah. Because Nathan of Gaza had convinced so many that Sabbatai Zevi was truly the Messiah, the Jews of Smyrna were now ready to accept Sabbatai as their savior. Thus, the assembled multitude in the synagogue shouted, "Long live our King, our Messiah."

The enthusiasm over Sabbatai Zevi was by no means confined to Smyrna. Jewish communities all over Europe believed that Sabbatai Zevi was the Messiah. Thousands of Jews sold their homes, and made ready to follow the new Messiah on what they believed would be his triumphant return to the Holy Land.

But these high hopes were soon to be shattered. Sabbatai set sail for Constantinople, expecting that the Sultan would pay homage to him. Upon his arrival there, he was detained by the Sultan's officers. Not knowing what to do with him, and fearful of making him a martyr by executing him, the Sultan threw him into prison. In prison, thousands came to visit Sabbatai, and his influence spread.

But there were opponents to his Messianic claim among his own people. A Polish Jew named Nehemiah Cohen came to visit Sabbatai. Unconvinced of Sabbatai's mission, Nehemiah Cohen denounced Sabbatai as a traitor. This information was conveyed to the Sultan. A council of state was convoked. At this council, it was decided to send the Sultan's physician to Sabbatai. This physician was an apostate Jew: a Jew who had converted to Islam. He advised Sabbatai to convert to Islam, in order to save himself. Now in danger of his life, Sabbatai followed the advice of the Sultan's physician. Sabbatai Zevi took off his Jewish garments and donned the Turkish turban, signifying his adherence to the Moslem faith. Sabbatai left the Sultan's presence as Mehemet Effendi, his Turkish Majesty's "keeper of the palace gates."

Surprisingly, this was not the end of the Sabbatian movement. Instead of seeing Sabbatai's conversion to Islam as an act of betrayal to Judaism, Nathan of Gaza looked upon it as the fulfillment of Sabbatai's mission: Sabbatai had merely gone over to Islam temporarily, to lift up the sparks of God's presence which were dispersed among the gentiles and concentrated now in Islam.

Nathan of Gaza believed that there are sparks of God that only the Messiah can discover and redeem. He also believed that the Messiah can redeem them only by descending deep into the *Kelippot*—the realm of sin and evil—and conquering the evil from within. This meant that Sabbatai Zevi had to take upon himself the shame of being called a traitor to his people as the last step of his Messiahship—in order to lift up the sparks of God dispersed among the Moslems. In doing this, Sabbatai Zevi was acting like a spy sent into the enemy camp in order to conquer evil from within. This was the way Nathan of Gaza explained Sabbatai Zevi's conversion to Islam.

In fact, however, Sabbatai Zevi's conversion to Islam was a tragic event to most of the Jewish world. The high hopes of the Jews for redemption were crushed. The Jewish masses were disappointed and disillusioned. The man they had believed to be the Messiah had converted to Islam!

Nevertheless, Nathan persevered in his interpretation of

Sabbatai Zevi's conversion. There were those who accepted his interpretation and who still continued to believe that Sabbatai Zevi was the Messiah. In fact, for virtually a hundred years after Sabbatai's death, there were groups of Jews who continued to believe that he had been the Messiah.

Nevertheless most of the Jews, the Rabbis in particular, now realized that Sabbatai Zevi was not the Messiah and that Nathan was not the prophet of the Messiah. Nathan was excommunicated and expelled from many of the cities he visited, in his effort to spread Sabbatianism. He returned to Turkey and died there, in the city of Sofia, in 1680.

After his conversion to Islam, Sabbatai Zevi himself led a double life. Despite the fact that he had converted to Islam, he secretly would still chant psalms and teach the *Zohar* before a small gathering of his Jewish friends. He was once discovered by the Moslems in the act of singing psalms and was banished to Dulcigno, a small town in Albania where he died in 1676.

Thus ended the career of that strange man who, at one point in history, was hailed by many Jews as the Messiah.

Reflection

We learn something about human nature from the life of Sabbatai Zevi. There is a tendency in people, especially when times are bad, to look to one man who will be their savior, their Messiah. And even when this man appears to fail in his mission, his followers will try to explain the seeming failure as part of his mission.

This is what happened in the case of Sabbatai Zevi. Despite his conversion to Islam, his leading disciple—Nathan of Gaza—interpreted what he did as part of his mission: Sabbatai converted, according to Nathan, to discover and lift up the sparks of God among the gentiles.

There is some similarity here to the Christian belief in Jesus as the Messiah. The crucifixion and death of Jesus, who died as a criminal, was certainly a blow to his disciples. Yet they continued to believe that he was the Messiah, was resurrected from the dead and would return at the time of his second coming.

The *Kabbalah*, of all the traditions within Judaism, had the most exalted concept of man. Man, according to the Kabbalah, was responsible for *Tikkun*—for the mending and healing of God's world. One can therefore understand why it was that the *Kabbalah* allowed belief to arise in a supernatural Messiah—a belief that one man had the mystical power to save the Jewish people.

Sabbatai Zevi offered hope to many Jews at a terrible time in their history. But when it became clear that the answer to their problems did not lie in a supernatural Messiah, Jews looked for another kind of mystical leader.

The mystical leader who seemed to offer the best hope for the Jews was the Baal Shem Tov. Here was a new type of leader, preaching a new idea of the pious man—the *Hasid.*

Let us now find out who the Baal Shem Tov was.

9

The Baal Shem Tov

At the end of the seventeenth century, the Jews of Poland were in
a depressed spirit. Between the years 1648-1658, approximately
100,000 Polish Jews had been killed by the Ukranian cossacks.
Sabbatai Zevi's conversion to Islam in 1666 had disillusioned most
of the Jewish people, except for Sabbatai's most ardent followers.
Talmudic learning was at a low ebb. There was a general apathy
toward learning of any kind. This indicated a decline in the quality
of Jewish life. What was needed was a new kind of leader, a man
who could arouse the spirit of his fellow Jews with a new message.
Such a man was the Baal Shem Tov.

Who Was the Baal Shem Tov?
At this time in Poland, there were many folk-healers who were
believed to possess magical powers. People believed that these
folk-healers could cure the sick by invoking a name of God. Thus,
these folk-healers were called *Baale-Shem:* Masters of the Name of
God.

But the Baal Shem Tov was no ordinary folk-healer. He came to
be known as the Baal Shem *Tov*—the Master of the *Good* Name.
By invoking the sacred name of God he was able to heal not only a
person's spirit, but also his body. He gained the confidence of the
people through his true piety. Thus he was called the Master of
the *Good* Name.[1]

What was his original name? And how did he achieve such a
remarkable reputation?

The original name of the Baal Shem Tov was Israel ben Eliezer.

He was born around 1700 in Okop, a small town in a section of Poland called Podolia.[2] Orphaned as a child, he was educated by the community. But Israel did not like to stay indoors and study. He rebelled against the dark, damp and depressing atmosphere of the Heder—the one room school. He preferred to escape into the woods and commune with nature.

At the age of twelve he became a helper to the schoolmaster. He gathered the children from their homes in the morning and took them back in the evening. On the way he taught them the songs of the synagogue. His enthusiasm—one of his most important traits—was felt by the children, who sang with great intensity.

When he was fourteen, he became a Shamash or "beadle" of the little synagogue in his village community. At night, in the stillness of the synagogue, it was said that he meditated on the mysteries of the *Zohar*. His interest was in the *Zohar*—in mysticism—and not in learning the Talmud.

The fact that he was not a Talmudic scholar did not earn him the respect of his future brother-in-law, Rabbi Gershon Kitiver. Rabbi Gershon advised his sister, Hannah, against marrying Israel—who appeared to be only a primitive, clumsy peasant. But Hannah went against her brother's wishes and married Israel ben Eliezer.

The years that followed were hard for Israel and Hannah. Rabbi Gershon was ashamed of his brother-in-law and persuaded the couple to go as far away as possible. He bought them a horse and cart, and sent them on their way.

In his twenties, Israel and his wife Hannah thus went to live in an isolated region of the Carpathian Mountains. There they worked the soil and eked out a living by digging lime, which they sold in town. Materially, their life was one of great poverty. But spiritually, their life was rich.

Virtually every great religious leader came forth with his message only after long periods of meditation in lonely places: Moses in the wastes of Midian, Buddha in the loneliness of the Ganges, Mohammed in the Arabian wilderness. The Baal Shem Tov was no different. In the solitude of the Carpathian Mountains, Israel ben Eliezer found his God. The ideas of a new religious movement began to take shape in his mind. Finally, at the age of thirty-six, Israel revealed himself as a leader. He began to teach the principles of a new religious way—Hasidism—which was to become a popular Jewish mystical movement.

Hasidism

The Hebrew word "Hasid" means a pious man.

In the history of Judaism, piety had always been associated with learning. Thus, Hillel, a first century Rabbi, had taught in the *Ethics of the Fathers:* "Nor can an ignorant person be truly pious."[3]

The Baal Shem Tov's message was different. He taught that an individual did not have to be learned or aristocratic to be religious. God can be approached and worshipped by all his creatures—by the ignorant as well as the learned, by the poor as well as the rich.

The times were ripe for this teaching of the Baal Shem Tov. The times were ripe for a leader like the Baal Shem Tov, who inspired the people with the feeling that all of them were loved by God, regardless of learning or social status.

This, then, was the first principle of Hasidism: Judaism is a democracy. Every Jew, no matter how simple or uncultured, could be pious.

And the Baal Shem Tov was a living example of this Hasidic principle:

> The Baal Shem was a man of the people in the true sense of the word. He could not claim a notable ancestry, nor did he occupy an exalted social position; nothing linked him to the ruling class. He had no official titles, no influential friends, no powerful protectors. He had neither material possessions nor wealthy admirers. He could not even lay claim to vast Talmudic learning. . . . This partly explains his immediate success among the less fortunate—they identified with him.[4]

This was the source of the Baal Shem's leadership: the ordinary Jew was able to identify with him. The Baal Shem Tov convinced the poor, simple Jew that he was a unique individual, a part of his people's destiny and infinitely precious to God.

Hasidic Tales and Teachings

The culture of Hasidism is expressed through its tales, its stories. The tales of the Hasidim convey the oral tradition of Hasidism.

The tales serve many functions. They are a record of the history of the Hasidic movement. They describe the mystical piety of the Hasidic leaders. They serve as a guide to conduct.[5]

We can learn about the impact of the Baal Shem Tov and the teachings of his Hasidic movement through these tales. We can see from various Hasidic sayings and tales, what values and ideals the Baal Shem Tov wished to teach in his new movement.

Person to Person

A disciple secretly wrote down all the teachings he had heard from the Baal Shem. . . . [When] the Baal Shem knew that some one was secretly setting down in writing what he said. He gathered all his people around him and asked: "Who of you is writing down what I teach you?"

The disciple who had been taking notes said it was he, and brought the master what he had written. The Baal Shem studied it for a long time, page for page. Then he said: "In all this, there is not a single word I said. You were not listening . . . and your ears heard what I did not say."[6]

The Baal Shem Tov did not put his teachings in writing. He opposed the attempts of others to do so. Nevertheless, twenty years after his death in 1760, his disciple, Yaakov Yosef of Polonnoye, wrote down these teachings. The Baal Shem valued person-to-person communication more than the written word. He preferred his disciples to listen to his spoken word. He feared that his disciples would be so intent on writing down his words that they would miss the immediate, direct emotional flavor of the face-to-face contact. Had he lived in the twentieth century, the Baal Shem would have opposed the use of a tape recorder to record his words.

The Baal Shem's concern, expressed in the above tale, emphasizes a central teaching of Hasidism: that a person is more important than the written word or a book. Religion is more than book knowledge.

The Baal Shem Tov wrote no books. It was, rather, the impact of his personality that led to the formation of a new movement in Judaism. And in Hasidism it was the personality of the religious leader—who came to be known as the *Zaddik*: the "perfected man", the "proven one", the "righteous one"—that was the highest motivating force.

This theme is expressed in the following saying, which was entitled: "To Say Torah And To Be Torah."

Rabbi Leib, son of Sarah, said this:

> I did not go to the *Maggid* [the Baal Shem's successor] in order to hear Torah from him, but to see how he unlaces his felt shoes and laces them up again.[7]

It was not the content of what the *Zaddik*—the Hasidic leader—said that was the most important thing. Most significant was being in the presence of a man whose heart had been touched and changed by God: the *Zaddik* did not merely teach Torah. He was a living Torah to his disciples.

The Baal Shem Tov, and his new movement, Hasidism, thus presented a new type of religious leader to the Jewish people. The traditional Jewish leader had been the scholar, the student of the Torah, the learned Rabbi. In place of the teacher of the Law, Hasidism gave birth to a new type of leader—the *Zaddik*—the perfected man, whose heart had been moved and touched by God.[8]

What led to this concept of the "perfected man"? It was that underlying Jewish mystical belief in the potential holiness of man—the belief that the purpose of God's creation of the world was to give birth to the *Zaddik*—the man who had perfected his soul and had thus become a holy man.

The Deaf Man

Rabbi Moshe Hayyim Efraim, the Baal Shem's grandson told:

> I heard this from my grandfather: Once a fiddler played so sweetly that all who heard him began to dance, and whoever came near enough to hear, joined in the dance. Then a deaf man who knew nothing of music, happened along, and to him all he saw seemed the action of madmen—senseless and in bad taste.[9]

To the Baal Shem Tov, Judaism was a joyous religion. The Baal Shem Tov was like the fiddler, inviting his fellow Jews to join in a joyous dance—Hasidic Judaism.

Unfortunately, the enemies of Hasidism saw Judaism purely as the study of Torah and as prescribed observances. They were like the deaf man, who could not understand the joy and enthusiasm of the dancers because he could not hear the music. In contrast to them, the Baal Shem taught that prayer and observance of the commandments without *Kavanah*—the right intent and a joyous spirit—were like a body without a soul.

The Besht lived at a time when Jewish life in Poland was permeated with sadness, due to the aftermath of the Cossack massacres and the internal decline within Jewry itself. The Baal Shem emphasized joy to counteract their depressed spirit:

> He taught them to fight sadness with joy. "The man who looks only at himself cannot but sink into despair, yet as soon as he opens his eyes to the creation around him, he will know joy." And this joy leads to . . . God; that was the new truth as defined by the Baal Shem. And Jews by the thousands let themselves be carried by this call, they needed it to live and to survive.[10]

Joy and enthusiasm in prayer and in life—this was the way of the Baal Shem Tov. The Jew did not have to undergo excessive fasting and self-torture to serve God, as many other religious mystics taught.[11] God desired the joyous heart, the enthusiastic fulfillment of the commandments, the flaming fervor of the pious man at prayer who sees every moment of life as a new gift of God.

Such joy—being inflamed with enthusiasm for God—*Hitlahavut* was the emphasis of the Baal Shem Tov.

How Ahijah Taught Him

The rav of Polonnoye told: At first the Baal Shem did not know how to talk to people, so wholly did he cling and cleave to God, and he talked softly to himself. Then his God-sent teacher Ahijah, the prophet, came and taught him which verses of the Psalms to say every day, to gain the ability of talking to people without disrupting his clinging to God.[12]

An important concept of Hasidism is *Deveikut*—cleaving unto God. The teaching of Hasidism is that "God can be beheld in each thing and reached through each pure deed . . . for no thing can exist without a divine spark."[13] God, to the Hasid, can be found everywhere—in nature and in the soul of a peasant. There is a spark of holiness in all things. Man's task is to continually search for this Divine spark in all things—to perpetually seek God—to desire to cling and cleave to Him at all times.

Mystics throughout the ages have sought God in solitude. They believed that they had to be alone—away from society, apart from other people—to discover God. In the history of mysticism, most mystical journeys were taken by individuals who withdrew from society.

Until his thirty-sixth year, the Baal Shem Tov, alone in the Carpathian Mountains, had sought and discovered God. Now he saw his task as that of bringing heaven to earth.[14] His desire was to teach his new message about God to the people.

His problem, however, was how to talk to people without disrupting his cleaving to God. How could he remain faithful to his own quest for God and at the same time mingle with people? Would he himself lose his fervor if he attempted to spread his message into the community? Could he really bring his heavenly message to earth?

The Besht needed God's inspiration to solve this problem. According to a Hasidic tale, God sent a vision of the prophet

Ahijah to the Baal Shem. Ahijah taught him Psalms as a way of reassuring him that he could bring the message of Hasidism to the community and still remain faithful to his own inner light.

How did the Besht spread the message of Hasidism? And how did Hasidism develop after he died?

These are some of the questions we shall examine in Part IV.

Reflection

We can look at the main events in the life of the Baal Shem Tov as historically true but embellished by legends, such as that of the vision of the prophet, Ahijah. The lives of the founders of all great religious movements are surrounded by legends. So, too, was the life of the Baal Shem Tov—the founder of Hasidism. Why is this so?

Mankind needs the image of the individual "perfected man" as a guide, as a model, as someone to imitate, as a pattern to follow. It is this need that creates legends and tales of great religious leaders.

Jewish mysticism, we have seen, exalts the position of man in the world. Man—especially "the perfected man," the *Zaddik*—is the purpose of God's creation. So it is not difficult to understand why the image of the Baal Shem Tov—the founder of Hasidism— has been adorned with legends.

Were the successors of the Baal Shem Tov faithful to his image? Did they live up to the ideal of the *Zaddik* as set forth by the Baal Shem Tov? Could the Kabbalistic image of man stand the test of reality?

It is to the practical, realistic effects of Jewish mysticism on earth, in the everyday world, in the community, and into modern times that we now direct our attention.

Part Four

EARTH

10

Mysticism For the Masses

The Baal Shem Tov "brought heaven down to earth."[1] He had spent many years of his life in retreat in the Carpathian Mountains. There, secluded from society, he discovered his way to God. When he returned to society at the age of thirty-six, he came with his new message of Hasidism.

But how was he to spread this message? He needed helpers to join him in his work. He needed disciples; students and followers who would assist him in teaching the masses of Jews about Hasidism.

Eventually, a circle of followers gathered around the Baal Shem Tov. Who were his helpers? Who were his successors? What was their relationship to the community? And what was the practical effect of Hasidism on the masses of Jewry?

Rabbi Yaakov Yosef

Yaakov Yosef was the Rabbi in Sharogrod and later in Polonnoye, both provinces of Poland. Born of a family of scholars, he was steeped in Talmudic learning. He had heard of the Baal Shem Tov, but he did not believe in his message. Yaakov felt that learning was more important than joy. In fact, we can picture Yaakov Yosef as a harsh, stern man, very strict in his observance of Jewish ritual and very devoted to the study of Torah. He was aloof from the people of his community and their problems and quick tempered in his reactions to others.[2] In these traits, Yaakov Yosef was the typical Rabbi of the times—immersed in study and his own concerns and indifferent to the needs of his people. It was precisely as a contrast to this type of Rabbi that the Baal Shem

Tov set forth his ideal of the *Zaddik*—the "perfected man" and the
true leader of his people.

The Baal Shem Tov knew about Rabbi Yaakov Yosef. He felt
that he could help Rabbi Yaakov to change and become a *Zaddik*.
It was with this intention in mind that the Baal Shem Tov went to
Sharogrod to visit Rabbi Yaakov Yosef.

The custom in Sharogrod was to commence morning prayers at
eight o'clock. The sexton generally opened the synagogue at six-
thirty. When the Baal Shem came to Sharogrod, however, he
went to the market place and began to attract people by telling
stories. Even the sexton of the synagogue stopped to listen to his
tales.

When Rabbi Yaakov Yosef came to synagogue that morning, he
found it locked. Because of his short temper, he became angry
over the delay.

The sexton finally came to open the doors of the synagogue.
When Rabbi Yaakov saw him, he asked him why the men who
usually came to the service were not there. The sexton told him
that a certain stranger was standing in the market place telling
stories and that everyone, including the men who usually came to
the service, had gathered around him to listen. Overcome with
anger, Rabbi Yaakov Yosef was forced to pray alone.

When he finished praying, Rabbi Yaakov Yosef ordered the sexton to bring the visiting storyteller to him, in order to have him
flogged for delaying the morning service. When the Baal Shem arrived, Rabbi Yaakov asked him indignantly, "Are you the one
who delayed the service?" The Baal Shem answered, "Rabbi, I am
the one." The Baal Shem continued, "I request your eminence
not to be angry with me. Let me tell you a story." Rabbi Yaakov
Yosef listened to the story and was deeply moved by it. He was no
longer angry.

The Baal Shem continued to tell his stories to Rabbi Yaakov
Yosef. After the third story, Rabbi Yaakov felt drawn to the Baal
Shem.

Then the Baal Shem said, "I have not prayed yet. I wish to go
and pray." While he prayed, Rabbi Yaakov prepared a meal for

him. After the meal, the two men walked and talked together. The people of Sharogrod followed after them and saw what was happening. The Baal Shem Tov had drawn their Rabbi to him. From this time forth Rabbi Yaakov Yosef was a disciple of the Baal Shem Tov.[3]

The Baal Shem Tov taught Rabbi Yaakov Yosef to love all Jews—the unlearned and the sinners as well as the learned and righteous. He impressed upon Yaakov Yosef that at this time of crisis, the Jewish community needed dedicated leaders who would not stand aloof from the people but rather would go out to them in love and raise them up to a higher spiritual level. Thus the Baal Shem taught Yaakov Yosef the importance of *Ahavas Yisrael—* love of the Jewish people. He also taught him that God wants man to serve Him in happiness and joy, not in sadness and gloom. The Baal Shem Tov visited Rabbi Yaakov again and again, and completely won him over to the way of Hasidism.

So moved and changed was Rabbi Yaakov Yosef by the Baal Shem Tov that he wrote the first Hasidic book—*Toldot Yaakov Yosef.* This book appeared in 1780, twenty years after the death of the Baal Shem Tov, and is still one of the main sources of the teachings of the Baal Shem.

In his book, Rabbi Yaakov Yosef described what he learned from the Baal Shem Tov about the task of the Jewish leader and his relationship to the community.

According to Rabbi Yaakov, there was a gap between the Rabbis and their communities. The Rabbis were too concerned about their own learning, their own personal security and their own pride and authority. They had become aloof from their people. Rabbi Yaakov Yosef was obviously describing the way he was before he met the Baal Shem.

The task of the true Jewish leader, Rabbi Yaakov said, is to bring his people closer to God. The Torah had become meaningless for many of the people and the *Mitzvot* were performed mechanically. The Jewish leader had to ignite a spark—to restore the desire in the people to seek God. How was he to accomplish this?

The leader had to perfect himself first. He had to become a humble servant of God, willing to sacrifice himself for his people. This was the first goal of Hasidism—to create a new kind of leader: the *Zaddik*. The *Zaddik* was to be the perfected man who serves God in the midst of the community. No longer was Jewish mysticism to be a secret; a mystery guarded by the chosen few. *Hasidism was Jewish mysticism brought down to earth.* The task of the *Zaddik* was to transmit his awareness of God to the people, to make it known to people. His task was to bring heaven to earth, to raise the people from earth to heavenly spiritual heights.

Having dedicated himself completely to God and His service, the *Zaddik* was to become a spiritual helper to his people. This meant that the *Zaddik* was to help his people to communicate with God:

> The Zaddik must make communication with God easier for his hasidim, but he cannot take their place . . . He develops the hasid's own power for right prayer, he teaches him how to give the words of prayer the right direction, and he joins his own prayer to that of his disciple and therewith lends him courage. . . .[4]

Yaakov Yosef, like the Baal Shem Tov, did not teach the people to depend completely upon the *Zaddik*. The *Zaddik*, as conceived by the Baal Shem and by Yaakov Yosef, was to help his people communicate with God. He was not, at this early stage of Hasidism, conceived of as one who prayed for the people and who represented them before God. The important thing was the relationship between the *Zaddik* and his community. This relationship was intended to be one of love and unity between the helper and his disciples.

To create this relationship, Rabbi Yaakov Yosef established the first Hasidic house of worship in Sharogrod. This paved the way for the founding of separate synagogues for Hasidim—an important step in the growth of the Hasidic movement. In his writing and in his activity as a leader, Rabbi Yaakov Yosef thus played an important role in the development of Hasidism.

The Maggid of Mezeritch

The Baal Shem Tov did not choose Rabbi Yaakov Yosef as his successor. We do not know exactly why he was not chosen. Perhaps the Baal Shem, before his death, changed his mind about putting his teachings into writing. Perhaps he realized that it was necessary for Yaakov Yosef to have the time to write about and record his teachings and tales for future generations. Perhaps he thought that Yaakov Yosef was too intellectual for the majority of Jews.

Instead of Rabbi Yaakov Yosef, the Baal Shem chose as his successor Rabbi Dov Baer of Mezeritch, a gifted "Maggid" (preacher) and an outstanding organizer. After the death of the Baal Shem Tov in 1760, Dov Baer became the leader of the Hasidim. Under his leadership, the movement grew and spread. Just as Nathan of Gaza was the organizer for and spread the message of Sabbatai Zevi's "Messiahship," so Rabbi Dov Baer became the great organizer of the Hasidic movement.

Within the space of twelve years, the "Maggid" succeeded in establishing a Hasidic network spanning all of Eastern Europe. Because of the "Maggid," the Baal Shem Tov's message of Hasidism was made available to widely dispersed communities. The "Maggid" was a brilliant administrator. He divided Central Europe into various regions. He assigned a Hasidic Rebbe—a *Zaddik*—to each community. The title "Rebbe" was a Yiddish word used to distinguish the Hasidic leader from the traditional Rabbi, who was often referred to as the "Rav," or the master of learning.

The "Maggid," himself a skillful preacher, trained the Rebbes in the art of public speaking. He gave some excellent practical advice for speakers: "Whenever you deliver an address stop before the end, before you have said it all."⁵ In this way, the speaker leaves the audience with a desire to hear more, and to hear him speak again.

But the emphasis of Rabbi Dov Baer on the training of Zaddikim and the spread of the movement had its dangers. So intent was Dov Baer on the training of the Zaddikim that he focused his attention on them rather than on the Hasidim—their followers. The very thing that Yaakov Yosef feared—the excessive dependence of the Hasidim, the followers, on the Zaddikim, their leaders—came to pass. Dov Baer imbued the Zaddikim with a sense of their own powers. The Hasidim came to believe that the Zaddikim were indeed their representatives before God. Instead of the ideal of the *Zaddik* as a helper—as Yaakov Yosef had written— the actual Zaddikim were all too often regarded by their followers as possessing godlike powers, being the intermediary between them and their God. This unfortunate tendency was known as Zaddikism or "the cult of the *Zaddik*" (the worship of the *Zaddik*).

Dov Baer thus magnified the concept of the *Zaddik* to a degree undreamed of by the Baal Shem Tov. The *Zaddik*, in the eyes of his followers, frequently became the representative of God upon earth, a kind of spiritual superman.

This excessive devotion to the *Zaddik* aroused the opposition of many non-Hasidic Rabbis. These antagonists of Hasidism were known as *Mitnaggedim*—opponents.

A ban against the Hasidic sect was issued in 1772 by the leader of the *Mitnaggedim*, Elijah, the Gaon of Vilna. He was the most prominent Talmudic scholar and Rabbinic authority of the time. Shortly thereafter, Dov Baer died, broken in spirit as well as in body.

The opposition to Hasidism gave rise to a decentralization of Hasidic leadership. Individual Hasidic leaders developed with their own patterns of leadership, and their own followers.

Saint-Mystics

Fortunately, there were many outstanding personalities among these leaders who kept Hasidism alive and vital during this period. Between the years 1750 and 1800, Hasidism produced a group of truly original religious leaders.

In 1772, following the death of the "Maggid" of Mezeritch, Hasidic leaders distributed the authority among themselves. They designated their sons or other close relatives as their successors. Thus, they created hereditary dynasties, some of which still continue to the present time. But the greatness of the movement was to be found in those Hasidic leaders who developed their own u- nique styles of interpretation and teaching. They were not only mystics, seeking the hidden presence of God in the world. They were also saints; their lives were an example of true religion in ac- tion. These saint-mystics were models of piety, authentic men of God. But each one offered a different teaching, a unique way to God.

Rabbi Levi Yitzhak

Among these saintly personalities was Rabbi Levi Yitzhak of Ber- ditchev (1740-1810), also known as the "Berdichever." He was a living example of *Abavas Yisrael*—love of the Jewish people. His love of his people was so great that he pleaded their cause before God. He even argued with God, calling God to a *Din Torah*—an accounting—because of the suffering of His chosen people.

These are the words of Rabbi Levi Yitzhak's *Din Torah* with God:

> How could I venture to ask You [Lord] why everything happens as it does, why we are driven from one exile into another, why our foes are allowed to torment us so. . . . I do not beg you to reveal to me the secret of your ways—I could not bear it! But show me one thing; show it to me more clearly and more deeply: show me what this, which is happening at this very moment, means to me, what it demands of me, what you, Lord of the world, are telling me by way of it. Ah, it is not why I suffer, that I wish to know, but only whether I suffer for your sake.[6]

Thus did Rabbi Levi Yitzhak of Berditchev seek meaning in his suffering, and in the suffering of the Jewish people. In this prayer, he was asking God to show him the purpose of Jewish suffering. But Rabbi Levi's question was a strange one. It was a question that he alone, and not God, could answer. He was actually questioning the justice of God, calling God to account: if the Jews were His people, why did they suffer?
Rabbi Levi Yitzhak did not set forth a theory, as Isaac Luria did,

to explain Jewish suffering. He asked a question. He realized that he had to find a meaning in his suffering, and the suffering of his people. He realized that other Jews would see different meanings in their suffering. To Rabbi Levi Yitzhak, the search for meaning was a personal one. Each Jew had to find it for himself. But what Jews had in common, Rabbi Levi Yitzhak thought, was the need to ask the question. In the prayer of Rabbi Levi Yitzhak of Berditchev, the question was more important than the answer.

Rabbi Nachman of Bratslav

Rabbi Nachman of Bratslav (1772-1811) was the great-grandson of the Baal Shem Tov. As a young man, he spoke to God, but he felt that God did not answer him. He fasted and prayed. He concentrated, hoping for a revelation from God. But nothing happened.

At the age of fourteen, he married and settled in the village where his father-in-law lived. In the village, away from the city, he learned to appreciate nature. It was his feeling for nature that made him aware of God. Thus, he taught the service of God through the awareness of the beauties of nature. He said to his disciples:

> When a man becomes worthy . . . to hear the songs of the plants, how each plant speaks its song to God, how beautiful and sweet it is to hear their singing! And, therefore, it is good indeed to serve God in their midst in solitary wandering over the fields between the growing things and to pour out one's speech before God in truthfulness.[7]

From the village, he went to a small town where he instructed people in his teachings. He could have become like many other Zaddikim of his time—taking advantage of the admiration of their disciples, and acquiring fame and profit. But Rabbi Nachman saw in this "cult of the *Zaddik*" the decline of Hasidism. He tried to prevent this decline by being a true *Zaddik*, like his grandfather, the Baal Shem Tov.

Rabbi Nachman tried to be a true *Zaddik* by drawing close to his people and really feeling their suffering. In this spirit, he related:

In the beginning . . . I wished of God that I might suffer the pain and need of Israel. But now, when one person tells me his pain, I feel the pain more than he does. For he can think other thoughts and forget the pain, but not I.[8]

Like Rabbi Levi Yitzhak, Rabbi Nachman was a true *Zaddik*—a saint-mystic. He suffered when his people suffered. He felt their pain. He was not only a mystic who felt the presence of God. He was a saint-mystic, who lived for his people as well as his God.

There were other saintly characteristics of Rabbi Nachman. In Bratslav, he taught and gathered many followers. But there were Zaddikim who opposed his views and who hated him. Rabbi Nachman, however, looked for the good even in his enemies. This is a true mark of the saint, the holy man.

After five years in Bratslav, Rabbi Nachman fell ill with consumption. During the last years of his life, he told his disciples many fables and tales so that they would remember concrete examples of his teachings. Even as he died, Rabbi Nachman showed his saintly character. He was not afraid to die, he said, because he had faith that after he died, his soul would live in eternity with God.

Reb Zusya

Reb Zusya of Hanipol also showed his saintly character in his ability to accept suffering and death.

Zusya was afflicted with blindness toward the end of his life. Most people react to blindness by asking, "Why has God done this to me? Why must I suffer? Why me?"

Reb Zusya's response, in contrast, was one of acceptance. He offered up this prayer:

"Thank you, O Lord, for making me blind so that I might see the inner light."[9]

Reb Zusya's prayer is an example of religious awareness—the ability to discover the sacred in the world. So saintly was Zusya that, even when afflicted with blindness, he still searched for the sacred in life.

Even as he approached the end of his life, his greatest fear was not death. Rather, his fear was whether he had made the most of his life, whether he had fulfilled his true value, his true worth in life:

> The students of Reb Zusya, hearing that their teacher was about to die, came to pay him one last visit. But entering the room, they were surprised to see him trembling with fear.
> "Why are you afraid of death?" they asked. "In your life, have you not been as righteous as Moses himself?"
> "When I stand before the throne of judgment," Zusya answered, "I will not be asked, Reb Zusya, why were you not like Moses? I will be asked, Reb Zusya, why were you not Zusya."[10]

The way to become a Hasid is not by copying others. It is by developing the goodness in our own unique personalities. The true *Zaddik* tried to develop this goodness in his Hasidim.

Reflection

What effect did Hasidism have on the Jewish communities of Eastern Europe? How did this popular mysticism affect the lives of the Jewish people?

Everything depended on the character of the *Zaddik*—the Hasidic leader. If he was a true *Zaddik*, an authentic Hasidic leader, he would inspire his individual Hasidim to develop their own religious awareness, their own way of worshipping God and their own special talents and abilities. The Hasid learned by the example of the true *Zaddik*. He learned love of the Jewish people from Rabbi Levi Yitzhak. He learned to appreciate nature from Rabbi Nachman of Bratslav. He learned how to accept suffering from Reb Zusya. These true Zaddikim—the saint-mystics who lived according to the ideals of the Baal Shem Tov—raised the level of piety of the masses.

But there were Zaddikim who abused the power of their position. They were Zaddikim in name only. They were not true Zaddikim. They used their position to acquire fame, riches and power. They allowed their followers to regard them as mediators between man and God. They caused their followers to commit the sin of idolatry; the sin of considering a human being to be as sacred as God. But their followers were equally to blame, because they allowed themselves to be dependent on the *Zaddik*.

This negative aspect of Hasidism—the cult of the *Zaddik*—was one of the factors that led to the rise of the *Mitnaggedim*, the opponents of Hasidism.

But the Hasidim and the *Mitnaggedim* eventually had to face a common enemy, the *Maskilim*. The *Maskilim* were the Jewish secularists. They believed that modern secular culture was more important than traditional Judaism. The Hasidim and the *Mitnaggedim* came together to preserve traditional Judaism.

What was the essence of East European Hasidism? In what forms does it survive in America today? To these and other related questions we now direct our attention.

11

The Hasidic Way of Life

Hasidic culture in Eastern Europe represented a joyous spiritual experience, exemplifying to all the world the deepest spirituality of Jewish life. How ironic and tragic it was, therefore, that so much of this lofty culture was destroyed by the Nazis during the Second World War in their mass murder of six million Jews. But the Nazis could not annihilate the spark—the Hasidic way of life. Those Hasidic Jews who survived World War II kept the spark alive in Hasidic communities in Israel, England, France, Holland, Italy, Canada and America.

What was the "spark" of East European Hasidism? In what forms does it survive in America today? What is the contemporary Hasidic way of life? And can the modern American Jew learn a new way of living from Hasidic spirituality?

The Spark

According to Hasidic tradition, the Baal Shem Tov once said:

> Do you want to know what Hasidism is? Do you know the story of the ironmonger who wanted to become independent? He bought an anvil, a hammer and bellows and went to work. Nothing happened— the forge remained inert. Then an old ironmonger, whose advice he sought, told him: "You have everything you need except the spark." That is what Hasidism is: the spark.[1]

This Hasidic "spark" is precisely what is missing in much of contemporary American Jewish life. Dr. Abraham J. Heschel, the

late Professor of Jewish Ethics and Mysticism at the Jewish
Theological Seminary (and who was also a descendant of the
famous Hasidic Rebbe of Apt) deplored the lack of fervor at services in many contemporary American synagogues:

> Services are conducted with dignity and precision. The rendition of
> the liturgy is smooth. Everything is present: decorum, voice, cere-
> mony. But one thing is missing: Life. . . . The fire has gone out of our
> worship. It is cold, stiff, and dead. . . . Who knows how to kindle a
> spark in the darkness of the soul? . . . The modern temple suffers from
> a *severe cold.* Congregants preserve a respectful distance from the liturgy
> and themselves. They say the words, "Forgive us for we have sinned,"
> but of course, they are not meant. They say, "Thou shalt love the
> Lord thy God with all thy heart" in lofty detachment, in complete
> anonymity as if giving an impartial opinion about an irrelevant ques-
> tion. . . . Assembled in the synagogue everything is there—the body,
> the benches, the books. But one thing is absent: soul.[2]

Heschel, in the foregoing passage, was writing out of the context
of his own Hasidic spirituality. It was this element of
spirituality—what the Hasidim call *Kavanah*—that Heschel found
lacking in the modern American synagogue. *Kavanah* means intense concentration on God when we pray and when we perform
a *Mitzvah*, a sacred deed or commandment. *Kavanah* is the inner
devotion, the feeling, the sacred intent that should accompany a
religious act. All too often, unfortunately, people read the prayer
book as they would peruse last night's newspaper. They are simply reading words. There is no soul, no spark in their worship.

Hasidism can serve as a model for a way of life, on the basis of
which we can examine our own spirituality—or lack of it. Two
descriptions of the spark of Hasidic spirituality convey to us what
may be missing in our own spiritual lives.

First, let us imagine what the Sabbath was like in the European
Hasidic community of Belz, in Galicia, Poland. Here is a descrip-
tion by Jiri Langer, a young man who went from Prague to visit
Belz in the early 1900s:

The Sabbath candles are already lit in the Rabbi's house. I enter with the other guests—there is a long queue of them—to greet the saint for the first time. . . .

He is a sturdy, tall, old man, with broad shoulders and an unusual, patriarchal appearance, dressed in a caftan of fine silk, wearing, like all the other men, a *shtreimel*, a round fur hat worn on the Sabbath, on his head, round which hang thirteen short sable tails of dark brown color. . . .

The spacious Belz synagogue has meanwhile filled with people. There are a hundred lighted candles. In a way the interior reminds me of the Old-New Synagogue in Prague. The men, for the most part tall and well-built, old and young, await the arrival of the rabbi, talking quietly among themselves. . . .

Dusk is already well advanced when the rabbi enters the synagogue. The crowd quickly divides to let him pass. Perhaps the waters of the Red Sea once divided in the same way before Moses.

With long, rapid strides he makes straight for the *bimah*, or reading desk, and the strange Chassidic service begins. . . .

It is as though an electric spark has suddenly entered those present. The crowd which till now has been completely quiet, almost cowed, suddenly bursts forth in a wild shout. None stays in his place. The tall black figures run hither and thither round the synagogue, flashing past the lights of the Sabbath candles. Gesticulating wildly, and throwing their whole bodies about, they shout out the words of the Psalm. They knock into each other unconcernedly, for all their cares have been cast aside; everything has ceased to exist for them. They are seized by an indescribable ecstasy. . . .

The sparks of the holy Wisdom of God, which fell into Nothingness when God destroyed the mysterious worlds that preceded the creation of our world, these sparks are now raised from the abyss of matter and returned to the spiritual Source from which they originally came.[3]

In this description of the Hasidic community of Belz, we see how the spark of Jewish mysticism came alive in the Hasidic community; the hush when the Rebbe entered the synagogue, the ecstasy as they began to pray and the belief that by their prayer, they were helping to raise the fallen sparks to God. The unity of the Rebbe and his Hasidim in Sabbath prayer—this is Jewish mysticism in action in the twentieth century.

Early in the twentieth century, another young man visited a Hasidic community. The young man was Martin Buber, the Jewish philosopher who was to become the foremost interpreter of Hasidism to the modern world. The Hasidic community was the village of Sadagora in Galicia. In his book *Hasidism and Modern Man,* Buber describes his visit, as a young man, to this Hasidic community:

> In my childhood (at a very young age, I came there from Vienna, where I was born, to Galicia and grew up there with my grandparents) I spent every summer at an estate in Bukovna. There my father took me with him at times to the nearby village of Sadagora. Sadagora is the seat of a dynasty of 'Zaddikim' (*Zaddik* means righteous, proven, completed), that is, of Hasidic rabbis. . . .
>
> This I realized at that time, as a child, in the dirty village of Sadagora from the 'dark' Hasidic crowd that I watched—as a child realizes such things, not as thought but as image and feeling—that the world needs the perfected man and that the perfected man is none other than the true helper. . . .
>
> The palace of the Rebbe, in its shadowy splendor, repelled me. The prayer house of the Hasidim with its enraptured worshippers seemed strange to me. But when I saw the Rebbe striding through the rows of the waiting, I felt 'leader,' and when I saw the Hasidim dance with the Torah, I felt, 'community.'[4]

It is instructive to compare Martin Buber's reaction to a Hasidic community with that of Jiri Langer. Both were impressed by the leadership of the Rebbe and the intense way the community responded to him. Both felt that Hasidism generated a feeling of true community; a sense of common joy and reverence, of oneness and brotherhood.

To be sure, Buber realized that the Rebbe often abused his power. Buber thus wrote: "Certainly, the power entrusted to him has been misinterpreted by the faithful, has been misused by himself."[5] Still, Buber thought, the negative aspects of the "cult of the Zaddik"—the excessive "Rebbe worship"—were overcome by the genuine help the Rebbe gave his followers.[6]

These European Hasidic communities of Belz and Sadagora, and the countless other Hasidic communities in eastern and central Europe would still exist today were it not for the cruelty and barbarity of the Nazis during the Second World War. The Hasidic world of eastern Europe ended in the Nazi concentration camps. The brutality of the Nazis—signifying the end of east European Hasidism—is described in this tragic account:

> The first day of Rosh Hashoneh I remember the Rabbi of the town and a group of Jews went to look for the Jews who were killed from the German bombs and were still lying under the houses. They were trying to take them out and bury them according to the Jewish law. The Rabbi announced that you were not allowed to daven in any shul on Rosh Hashoneh. He wouldn't allow any Jews to daven before we took care of those people who were buried underneath the houses. And that day already the Germans took all the group, and the Rabbi and my father were among them, and they took them to the market, and it was a big market, and they cut off their beards on one side of their faces to make it look awful. And they beat them. The Rabbi's clothes, I remember, they took off his clothes, rabbinical clothes, traditional, and they put it on one of the laymen. And they changed clothes—just to make him look ridiculous. And then they took his hat, his shtraiml, his Shabbes hat, a fur hat, and they collected garbage in it. And then the troubles began.[7]

The Nazis destroyed the Hasidic communities of Eastern Europe. But they could not destroy the spark of Hasidism.

An American Hasid

The spark of Hasidism is still alive; there is a wave of interest in Hasidism today by young Jews. There are Hasidic communities all over the world—in Israel, in England, France, Holland, Italy, Canada and America. We shall focus our discussion on Hasidism in America.

In America, there are numerous Hasidic communities: the Satmar Hasidim whose center is in Williamsburg, New York; the

Hasidim of the Bostoner Rebbe who meet at the New England
Hasidic Center in Brookline, Massachusetts; the Bobover Hasidim
in Brooklyn (Boro Park), New York; the Bratslaver Hasidim in
Brooklyn and the Squarer Hasidim in New Square, New York.[8]
However, "the most hospitable, the best organized, and the most
outgoing of all the groups,"[9] it has been contended, are the
Lubavicher Hasidim. It has been noted that "Lubavich is a highly
organized Hasidic community with branches all over the
world."[10] In America, there are branches of Lubavich in Alabama,
Arizona, California, Connecticut, Florida, Georgia, Illinois,
Maine, Maryland, Massachusetts, Michigan, Minnesota,
Missouri, Nebraska, New Jersey, New York, Ohio, Pennsylvania,
Rhode Island, Tennessee, Texas, Washington, Wisconsin, and
Virginia. The main center of the Lubavicher Hasidim is in
Brooklyn, New York.[11]

The Lubavicher Rebbe is Rabbi Menahem Mendel Schneerson.
He is the seventh Rebbe and a direct descendant of Rabbi Schneur
Zalman.

Rabbi Schneur Zalman (1748-1813) was born in Liadi in the
northern province of Lithuania, where the study of Torah and
Talmud were emphasized. He came to Mezeritch to hear the
Hasidic teachings of Rabbi Dov Baer, the great "Maggid" or
preacher. Inspired by the "Maggid," Schneur Zalman was "converted" to Hasidism. But he realized that the purely emotional
Hasidism that appealed to the simple folk of southern Poland
would not have the same attraction for the better educated Jews of
Lithuania. Rabbi Schneur Zalman therefore developed an intellectual version of Hasidism known as "Habad." "Habad" is an
acronym, standing for the initial Hebrew letters of *HOKHMAH*
(wisdom), *BINAH* (understanding) and *DAAT* (knowledge)—
which are also names of three of the *Sefirot* in the *Kabbalah*. Of all
types of Hasidism, "Habad" places the most stress on the study of
the Torah. But the uniquely Hasidic values of joy and *Kavanah*, or
inner devotion, and *Ahavas Yisrael*, love of the Jewish people are
still the main concepts stressed. How are these values integrated
into a coherent life-style? How and why are young Jews attracted

to Hasidism? To find out the answers to these questions, I met with Rabbi Yehoshua Laufer, a Lubavicher Hasid, and leader of a group of Hasidim in Providence, Rhode Island. Rabbi Laufer is thirty-one years of age, married, with five children.

The most noticeable thing about this Hasid is his radiant countenance. He exudes happiness. This is the unique characteristic of the Hasid: his joyous spirituality. I asked him about the Hasidic outlook on life. I wanted to know what is involved in the Hasidic world-view that brings to its followers this ineffable joy. He explained:

> The first principle of Habad "Hasidus" (spirituality) is *Ahavas Yisrael*—love of our fellow Jews. We all have the same *Neshama*—the same soul—given to us from our Father in Heaven. We consider all Jews as one organism: each Jew should consider his fellow Jew as if he were a part of himself. Our task as Hasidim is to bring out the soul of everything. By the 'soul' of everything, I mean *pinimiyus*—the inner essence of everything. We strive for inner understanding and appreciation. We believe that every person has a mission on earth. Every individual has a meaning and a purpose. No individual is worthless. Everyone is a child of God.
>
> We believe in *Kavanah*—that prayer and the *Mitzvot* (commandments) should be observed with deep, serious intent.
>
> In answer to your question about the source of Hasidic joy, let me tell you what the secret of happiness for a Hasid is. The word "Hasid" means "pious." Our constant search for inner understanding brings joy, for we discover God in everything. God is good. Therefore, everything in the world is good, or potentially good. Evil is only present as a challenge to be overcome, to be changed.[12]

At this point, I interjected. "Of course," I said, "some evils may be overcome. But some things cannot be overcome. For example, death is final, is it not?"

He replied, "A true Hasid does not fear death. When we die, we merely return our soul to our Creator. Our soul is that part of us which comes from God. It is present in every person."

"How do I know the soul exists?" I asked.

To this, the Hasid offered an interesting answer. Like the ancient Rabbis, the Hasidim recognize the existence of the *Yetzer HaRa*—the evil impulse. They refer to it as the "Animal Soul" as opposed to the "Divine Soul." The Hasidim believe that the purpose of the evil impulse is as a spur, an impetus, a challenge to be overcome. The *Yetzer HaRa*, Hasidim believe, is the source of our doubt and skepticism. "In order to have total belief in the Divine Soul and in God," the Hasid said, "we must conquer our *Yetzer HaRa*—our Animal Soul."

I was beginning now to see why Hasidism appealed to young people in search of a meaningful life-style and world-view. Here was a beautiful, spiritual way of life. According to this view, each person has a mission. The individual's purpose is to make the world a dwelling place for God—to allow the *Shechinah* (God's presence) to enter into our lives. But our selfish ego, our *Yetzer HaRa*, prevents us. We therefore must subdue it to let God in, and to keep our soul pure.

I realized why this Hasidic way of life appealed to the young; it not only offers them a purpose for their lives, but also leads them in search of truth, in search of authenticity, in search of a spiritual way of life.

After our discussion at his home, the Hasid and I went to the Hillel House of Brown University, where he taught a class in *Tanya*. *Tanya* is a famous philosophical work by Rabbi Schneur Zalman of Liadi, the founder of "Habad" Hasidism, in which the principles of this type of Hasidism are expounded.

There were three students waiting for Rabbi Laufer in the library of the Hillel House; Toni, Stuart, and David.

The Hasid began his discussion on the *Tanya* by explaining that Rabbi Schneur Zalman wrote this book for the "middle" people. The "middle" people—called in Hebrew "Benonim"—are those who are neither fully righteous nor totally wicked. They are the majority of us, for whom there is a constant struggle between the Divine *Neshama*—our godly soul, and our *Yetzer HaRa*, our animal soul—which tests us and tempts us to act selfishly rather than pursuing "Godliness."

Rabbi Laufer pointed out that "Hasidus" gives us insight into psychology. We have evil in us, but we can control it, we can channel it towards the good. We can extract good out of evil—for even evil is potentially good according to Hasidism.

A large part of the discussion dealt with the soul. Toni and Stuart believed in the soul. David was skeptical.

Toni described her experience when she recognized the existence of a "soul" within her. She talked about an experience she had one night in which she felt "plugged in" to God. It felt, she said, like being plugged into an electric socket. She experienced a sense of separation from her body. She saw a radiant light, she heard a beautiful sound. And she felt God's presence watching.

David expressed doubts about her experience. "How do you know," he asked, "that it wasn't merely a psychological trick?"

At this point, Stuart, a very sensitive young man, interjected: "Of course, you can't prove that she really experienced God and the soul. But you can't disprove it either. There is nothing wrong with skepticism. It is O.K. to have doubts. Skepticism is a useful tool. By using skepticism, a Hasid tries to make sure that he is not fooling himself. But spirituality is a very subtle thing. *There is a moment on a deep level when you and you only can bear witness.*"

This last statement of Stuart struck a responsive chord in me. To believe or not to believe in God and the soul—this is a personal decision. The individual—and the individual alone—can bear witness whether or not his experience is merely a psychological illusion or a real happening. There are no objective criteria to test the validity of a religious experience in the way that there are tests to determine the truth of a scientific experiment. In science, there are tests agreed upon by the scientific community. A religious experience, by contrast, is private. Each individual must bear witness. The authenticity of a religious experience can motivate the individual to what he believes is a better way of life.

A Hasid, to me, is not only a pious Jew. The word "Hasid" is related to the Hebrew word *Hesed*, which means lovingkindness. There is a kindness, a sweetness about Rabbi Laufer and his disciples. There is a glow, a radiance on their faces. They are kind, good people. A "Hasid" is not only one who observes Jewish law; he does more than that law requires. If moral character is a clue to determining whether these people really do have genuine religious experiences, I can accept the possibility that these people are "touched" by God.

Psychology cannot fully explain an authentic religious experience. The following words of the contemporary Christian monk and poet Thomas Merton express my feeling: "True contemplation is not a psychological trick but a theological grace."[13] What does this statement mean?

Contemplation and meditation are more than thinking. Contemplation is a gift of awareness, an awakening to the externally "Real." Meditation is a vivid awareness of God—the infinite Being—in the roots of our own inward, limited being. This is what the Hasidim mean by "soul." It is an echo of God; the "still, small voice" within us. Whether or not an individual can really experience it depends upon "theological grace"—it is a gift of God.

That afternoon at Brown University Hillel House, I saw twentieth century Hasidism in action. I saw the "outreach" of a Lubavicher Hasid—his appeal to these three young Jews to return to God and to Judaism.

This was not the only encounter I have had with Hasidim.

At Clark University, where I taught a course on Jewish mysticism some years ago, I saw the Lubavich "Mitzvah Mobile"—or "Mitzvah Tank"—on campus. There they tried to give concreteness to Hasidic spirituality in terms of Mitzvot; teaching Jewish college students the *Berachah*—the blessing—to say when putting on the *Tallis* (prayer shawl), how to put on *Tefillin* (phylacteries)—even how to erect a portable Succah. But most of all, what they communicated was what Rabbi Laufer conveyed to Stuart, Toni, and David—the ineffable joy of being a Jew.

Hasidic Joy
The Baal Shem Tov taught the Hasidim to fight sadness with joy:

The man who looks only at himself cannot but sink into despair, yet as soon as he opens his eyes to the creation around him, he will know joy.' And this joy leads to the absolute, to redemption, to God; that was the new truth as defined by the Baal Shem.[14]

Hasidim express joy through singing and dancing. They believe that through song and dance every Jew can rise above his physical limitations and experience the Godliness of his soul.

A unique Hasidic contribution to Jewish music is the *Niggun*—the song without words. The Hasidic *Niggun*—the wordless melody—can be joyous and ecstatic but is also pensive and reflective. It is melody freed from rigid formulas and rules. Feeling—the outpouring of heart and mind—is the inner core of the Hasidic melody. Words can limit pure melody. But without words, the melody can soar into the infinite. For this reason it has been said that in Hasidism, "melody is the pen of the soul."[15]

Hasidic joy is expressed even more ecstatically by dancing. To Hasidim, dancing is the way to express religious joy through the body. In Hasidic dancing, the entire body moves. The whole body, from head to toe, is absorbed in the joy of the dance. The verse from Psalms, "All my bones shall say: Lord, who is like unto Thee?"[16] is characterized in the Hasidic dance.

Hasidic dancing is always done by males and females separately, since mixed or social dancing is prohibited by orthodox Jewish law. There are two main types of Hasidic dancing—the *Mochol* or "circle" dance and the *Rikkud*—jumping or skipping up and down.

The *Mochol*, the circle dance, is done in a closed circle, with one hand, or both, resting on the shoulders of the dancer in front. The *Rikkud*, the up and down dance, is more often done in crowded quarters, where there is insufficient room for the circle dance. Individual Hasidim may perform a solo hopping dance, or it may be performed by two or more persons. The dancing is done to the rhythm of a lively Hasidic tune and is usually accompanied by hand clapping from the bystanders.[17]

Hasidic dancing is practiced on special occasions such as the

Festival of *Simchas Torah*—the Rejoicing of the Torah (celebrating the completion and beginning again of the reading of the Torah). On this joyous holiday, Hasidim dance with the scrolls of the Torah. Unlike the cold, spiritless, dutiful marching with the Torah which takes place in so many congregations today, the Hasidim dance together, with warmth, enthusiasm and fervor, truly rejoicing with the Torah. To the Hasidim, the Jew's attachment to Torah pulsates with joy—a joy which elevates the Jew above the pettiness of the mundane world.

Joy permeates Hasidic celebrations of other holy days also. On the Sabbath, Hasidim believe (according to the ancient Talmudic concept) that the Jew is endowed with an additional *Neshama*—a revitalized soul—which elevates him to a higher plane. The joy of this religious elevation is the spiritual culmination of every week. But this "extra" soul does not arise automatically. The Jew must prepare himself through *Kavanah* in prayer to receive this additional soul—this revitalization.

Thus, the emphasis on Shabbat praying is on *Kavanah*—cultivation of the proper intent, the proper feeling and the appropriate mood for prayer; bringing together one's scattered thoughts, purifying one's mind and heart, and making oneself a worthy instrument for the *Shechinah*—God's presence.

For the Hasidim, *Kavanah*—the concentration, the intent, the inner feeling takes precedence over *Keva*—the concept that prayer requires fixed times for its recital. In Hasidism, worship can be entirely spontaneous and informal. Thus, in their Shabbat praying, Hasidim may begin later and end later than other Jewish orthodox groups. The significant thing is not when the prayer is said, but *how* it is said. The essence of Hasidic prayer and celebration of Sabbaths and festivals is *Kavanah*.

Kavanah

No matter what aspect of Hasidism one is discussing, one always comes back to the central concept of *Kavanah*.

The Hasidic story is told of the shepherd boy who was so moved by the solemn blowing of the Shofar in the synagogue on

Rosh Hashanah that he responded in the only way he knew; he placed his fingers in his mouth and emitted a sharp, shrill whistle. The Hasidic master, Levi Yitzhak of Berdichev, regarded this as a true prayer, completely acceptable to the Lord. What counted was the *Kavanah*—the inner feeling, the intent. The importance of *Kavanah* is reflected in these Hasidic meditations on three Jewish holy days.

Rosh Hashanah, the Jewish New Year:

> On Rosh Hashanah the higher soul faculties are revealed. Quite simply, this means that the Jewish heart is more sensitive on this day, that every Jew feels more deeply his kinship with his Creator than during the rest of the year.[18]

What counts most on Rosh Hashanah—according to Hasidism—is that when the Jew affirms the Kingship of God, he must also feel more deeply his kinship with God. The emphasis is on *Kavanah*—the inner feeling.

Yom Kippur, the Day of Atonement, recalls the time when the High Priest entered the Holy of Holies to seek God's forgiveness for the sins of His people:

> On Yom Kippur each Jew must enter the Holy of Holies which is within himself. He must not think: "How can I enter when I am not dressed up." He must realize that to enter the Holy of Holies does not require dressing up, but rather simple, pure heartfelt thoughts.[19]

What counts is the *Kavanah*—the purity of feeling, thought and intent.

Passover, the Jewish Festival of Freedom, celebrates the Exodus from Egypt. The central observance of Passover is the *Seder*, the Passover meal, and the reading of the *Haggadah*, the Passover book. One section of the *Haggadah* is the story of the four sons: the wise son, the wicked son, the simple son and the one who does not know how to ask a question:

> While the four sons differ from one another in their reaction to the

Seder service, they have one thing in common: they are all present at the *Seder* service. Even the so-called 'wicked' son is there, taking an active, though rebellious, interest in what is going on in the Jewish life around him. This, at least, justifies the hope that some day the 'wicked' one also will become wise, and all Jewish children attending the Seder will become conscientious Jews, observing the *Torah* and Mitzvot.[20]

So the Hasidim believe that even in the wicked son—the rebellious son—there is a Divine spark that can be released if he is taught the proper *Kavanah*—the inner feeling and intent necessary to become a Hasidic Jew.

The Bostoner Rebbe

Rabbi Levi Yitzchak Horowitz, the Bostoner Rebbe, is the only American-born Hasidic leader in the world. He was born in Boston in 1921 and was educated in New York and Jerusalem, assuming his leadership in 1944. He is an heir of the Hasidic dynasties of Lelov and Nikolsburg, and ultimately traces his lineage back to the Yehudi of Pszysha, the Seer of Lublin, the Maggid of Mezeritch, and the Baal Shem Tov.

Rabbi Horowitz has transformed the classical role of the Rebbe to fit within the American social and cultural context. In so doing, he has created a vibrant and growing Hasidic community, including a significant number of university students and young professionals.

Having heard that many college students are attracted to Rabbi Horowitz's type of Hasidism, I visited with him to learn more about the variations in Hasidic leadership and Hasidic groups.

Rabbi Horowitz is a warm, gracious individual. He welcomed me into his study, a room filled with holy books. He sat down in his chair, stroked his long, gray beard and invited me to begin the discussion.

I explained to the Rebbe that I wished to learn about the underlying reasons for the variations between the types of Hasidic groups in America. He explained that the variations stem from the different places in Europe from which the groups originated and involve different approaches to and emphases on the Rebbe-Hasid relationship.

"In Polish Hasidism," Rabbi Horowitz explained, "the role of the Rebbe is to nurture the individual potential of each of his Hasidim. The Hasid uses the Rebbe as a mirror, within which he may glimpse his own potential greatness. The Rebbe discourages excessive dependence of the Hasidim on him. This individualization of the role of the Hasid culminated in the example of Rabbi Mendel of Kotzk, who actually drove away overly dependent Hasidim. It is this emphasis on the development of the potential of each Hasid which is stressed in Polish Hasidism—the type of Hasidism I represent."

"In contrast," the Rebbe continued, "Hasidim from Lithuania—such as the Lubavich and Karlin,—encourage stronger ties to the Rebbe. These Hasidim, for example, rely on their Rebbe for virtually everything in practically all areas of life. My Hasidim, however, come to me only for special concerns. The most rigid Hasidic groups, however, are those that come from Hungary, such as the Satmarer Hasidim. The Satmarer Hasidim have one of the largest followings in America. They maintain their original dress and their original customs. Of all the Hasidic groups in America, they are the most isolated and the least interested in adapting to the American way of life. Their ties to their Rebbe are very strong but do not necessarily cover all areas of decision-making."[21]

Rabbi Horowitz pointed out that the Satmar community (whose center is in the Williamsburg section of Brooklyn) is a very cohesive entity. They have their own schools: the Satmar *Kehilla* is responsible for the education of over 8,000 children. They maintain a weekly newspaper. They have their own welfare organizations, bakeries, butcher shops, and their own Burial Society. They are very community-minded even though they may not be reaching out.

The Bostoner Rebbe then went on to discuss his emphasis on

community involvement—on helping people. In a Hasidic role unique to him, the Bostoner Rebbe handles medical liaison and diagnostic referrals for Jews around the world wishing to utilize the superb medical facilities of Boston. Furthermore, hospitality is provided for those who accompany their sick relatives. The Rebbe's work as advisor and counselor to those in need is recognized throughout the world. Thus, Rabbi Horowitz, commenting on the different emphases of the various groups said, "The Bobover Hasidim emphasize song and dance, the Lubavicher Hasidim emphasize . . . fervor in prayer and Jewish learning, and we stress community involvement, with a blend of important aspects of the other groups."

The Bostoner Rebbe then went on to discuss his own personal philosophy of Hasidism.

"A Hasid," he said, "is a Jew who goes beyond the letter of the law. There is more spirit, more *Kavanah*, more preparation in his attitude toward the commandments. He gives something extra of himself to the service of God."

"The Baal Shem Tov," he continued, "once said that there are no 'doubles' in this world. Each person has his own special mission to perform. The proof of this is that each person's fingerprints are unique." Here, then, is another aspect of Hasidism that is significant; the concept of the uniqueness of each individual. The Baal Shem Tov tried to locate within each person a special quality, his unique potential—what that person, and *only* that person can contribute to the world. The revolutionary concept within Judaism that the Baal Shem Tov taught was that there is nothing or no one in this world that is not important. The tailor, the blacksmith, the shoemaker, the Talmudic scholar, each has a Divine spark. The Baal Shem Tov made the so-called common people feel that God cared about them. "So," the Bostoner Rebbe said, "in our concern for the other person, in our interest in the development of each person's true potential, in our outreach program to college students, and our communal involvement in terms of helping the sick and the troubled, we are following the original teaching of the Baal Shem Tov."[22]

I was extremely moved by the presentation of the Bostoner

Rebbe—especially by his concept that no person has a "double." The emphasis on the unique potential of every individual—and the Bostoner Rebbe's interest in helping the person to develop that potential—was an inspiring example to me of the vital spark ignited by an American-born Hasidic Rebbe.

Reflection: To Distill the Essence

Not everything about Hasidism, however, is positive. To the extent that their devotion to their Rebbe leads them to greater piety and good deeds, the Hasidic admiration for the Rebbe may be thought of as inspiring. The Rebbe's role as spiritual leader, as helper, and as counselor (as the Bostoner Rebbe perceives his role) is legitimate. But the admiration for the Rebbe, in Lubavicher circles for example, unfortunately tends toward "Rebbe worship," wherein the Rebbe is thought of as the intermediary between the Hasidim and God. This excessive veneration of the Rebbe may seem to border on idolatry. One can extract the essence of Hasidism—the spirituality, the joy, the *Kavanah*—without agreeing with all its emphases.

Furthermore, not all Hasidim display the *Ahavas Yisrael*—the love of the Jewish people—to the same degree as the Hasidim I have described. And there are various degrees of intensity in the life-styles of Hasidic groups.

Among the most intense are the Satmarer Hasidim of Williamsburg, New York. Unlike the Lubavicher Hasidim, who are open to many aspects of modern life, the Satmar Hasidim wish to shut out the modern, secular world. Television and movies are banned. Their goal is to maintain intense devotion to Judaism through social and intellectual isolation from the outside world.

Moreover, the Satmarer Hasidim are opposed to the State of Israel, for they believe that one is not permitted to restore the nation of Israel before the Messiah comes. They believe that the Jewish people should wait for salvation from God in the form of His promised Messiah rather than forging their own destiny.

We see, therefore, that not all Hasidic teachings, nor all Hasidic groups, relate to our contemporary world.

What we must do, therefore, is to distill the essence of Hasidism to discover those concepts and values of Hasidism which can make for a new way of living, a new spirituality. Viewing Hasidism as a springboard to spirituality, what can we learn from it to enhance our own spiritual life?

We learn, first of all, to do whatever we are doing with our whole being, with inner feeling and intent—with *Kavanah*. *Kavanah* can be applied to all our actions, not only to religious observances and prayer.

We can absorb, also, the Hasidic feeling of joy. Again, this need not be applied only to Jewish observances. It can be an attitude toward life and the world, the joy inherent in our universe. It is the feeling of the religious individual of being one with God. But even the non-observant Jew—indeed, even the non-believer—can experience the feeling of being one with the universe; the awareness that everything is a part of everything else.

Finally, we can distill from Hasidism the teaching that we are here on earth for a reason. No individual is worthless. Every individual, every thing, has a potential for goodness and for beauty. Hasidism can inspire us to cultivate the attitude that the world is basically good, that we are all participating in an enormous world-process that is essentially good.

Hasidism, in most of its manifestations, is a joyous, spiritual experience, which everyone can examine in order to further their own spirituality.

Hasidism can also be a powerful experience. It can change your life—as it transformed the life of the man who brought its message to the modern world. This man was the contemporary Jewish thinker, Martin Buber. We turn now to examine his experience with Hasidism in order to see other ways in which Hasidic insights can enhance our lives.

The poet Rilke said: "*You* must change your life." If you study Jewish mysticism with *Kavanah*—especially in its modern form of Hasidism—you may discover in your life a new meaning, a new depth, a new spirituality, and you may learn a new way of seeing the people and things in your world.

12

Martin Buber, Rav Kook and Contemporary Options

Mystics of every creed and race have described the progress of the spiritual life as a journey or a pilgrimage. Two contemporary Jewish thinkers have described in their writings their spiritual pilgrimage, their inner life, their yearning for God. One of these philosophers, Martin Buber, received spiritual enlightenment from Hasidism. The other, Rav Abraham Isaac Kook, late Chief Rabbi of Israel, was actually a literary mystic—describing in his writings the religious feelings he experienced in his quest for God.

Both of these men were philosophers. Both of them were familiar with modern science. By examining and understanding their reflections on their spiritual lives, we can gain insight into the issues raised in the beginning of this book.

As we began this study of the history and development of Jewish mysticism, we raised some philosophical questions. The focus of these questions was on knowledge and truth: can we, living in the twentieth century, believe that Jewish mystics "encountered" God? Is there another way of knowing besides the scientific way?

As infatuated as modern man is with scientific method and scientific technology, it is important to realize that science deals with phenomena which are subject to observable repetitive testing in a laboratory. Mysticism, by contrast, deals with the private, unique experiences of individuals. Clearly, we cannot use scientific method to measure what cannot be measured—the depths of human experience.

Religious reality is, therefore, a matter of perception, not proof. A gifted artist enables us to perceive the world in a different way:

a painter evokes a new way of seeing, a composer enriches the sounds we hear. Just as the artist perceives the everyday world in a different way, so the mystic experiences life in a new way. A mystic is an artist of the soul. He experiences life inwardly—with greater depth, intensity and spiritual sensitivity. He perceives an ultimate unity in all things—a oneness with the universe or with God. He feels cosmic joy—the very flowers and trees may sing to him of their Creator. He may see all reality as a symphony to God. He may feel himself to be a wave in the ocean of Being, part of the Cosmic process.

Now, even in an act of ordinary perception, we, in part, create the world we live in. Scientifically, what is "out there" are light waves and sound waves, atoms and molecules. But we do not see light waves, we do not perceive atoms. We see a red chair, we perceive a beautiful sunset. In actual life, therefore, "reality" is a joint product of the external world and our perception of it—what we bring to it. How much the more so is "spiritual reality" a joint product of the external world and the religious individual's perception of it.

Spiritually gifted people, such as Martin Buber and Rav Kook, bear witness through their experiences to a higher reality. Let us follow closely their articulation of their religious experiences. We cannot dismiss their experiences as subjective, because all reality—even our everyday perceptions—involves subjective elements. Reality is fluid, not fixed; total objectivity exists only for God. The "subjective" is therefore as much a part of "reality" as the "objective." What matters, therefore, is how we respond to the subjective testimony—the inner religious experience—of these thinkers. By sharing in their journey and intuitively responding to the experiences, ideas and feelings of these contemporary thinkers, we may gain a glimpse of another way of knowing and a Higher Divine Reality and Unity to be known.

Martin Buber and Hasidism

We begin with the life and thought of Martin Buber (1878-1965).

In our description of the Hasidic way of life, we noted Martin Buber's reaction as a young man to a Hasidic community. Looking back upon his early impressions of Hasidism, Buber wrote: "When I saw the Rebbe striding through the rows of the waiting, I felt 'leader' and when I saw the Hasidim dance with the Torah, I felt 'community.'"[1] These early impressions; the intense bond between the Rebbe and his followers, and the intensity of Hasidic spirituality, remained dormant in Buber until the age of twenty-six, when Hasidism opened to him a new way of looking at life. At the age of twenty-six, Buber withdrew into solitude for five years in order to study Hasidic literature. As a result of his study and his translation of Hasidic tales and legends, the Western world was acquainted with the Hasidic way of life.

Buber's treatment of Hasidism is of great significance because it opens up for modern man—as it did for Buber himself—a new and distinctive Jewish outlook on the world. Moreover, Buber's works on Hasidism offer an approach to Jewish spirituality for the Jew who wishes to be religious—who has deep religious feeling—but who cannot find the way to express these feelings in Jewish observances and rituals.

We will now trace the events of Buber's childhood and youth up to the age of twenty-six and explore the concerns that led him to his Hasidic "awakening".

Buber's Childhood

Martin Buber was born in Vienna on February 2, 1878. When he was three years old, his parents were divorced. Buber was not to see his mother again until he was thirty-three.

His separation from his mother at this early age had a searing effect upon his life. A cruel remark of an older playmate rendered this separation even more bitter to him. In a book of Buber's recollections of the formative influences in his life, he remarked that his earliest memory was of an event that occurred in the fourth year of his life—when an older child told him concerning his mother: "No, she will never come back."[2] Although Buber's meeting with his mother at the age of thirty-three proved this remark to be false, the four-year-old child intuitively understood it to be true.

Psychologists believe that the loss of the love of a mother at such an early age leaves a deep psychic wound and a lasting sense of insecurity in a child's mind. Clearly, the separation from his mother at age four shattered Buber's sense of security. Yet he was able to compensate for this by developing a special sensitivity to deep experiences: "As a sensitive child, Buber had developed an unusual aptitude for deep experiences, something in the nature of an additional sense, an antennalike organ of soul. . . . "³ This sensitivity became manifest early in his life.

After the divorce of his parents, Buber grew up in the home of his grandparents in Lemberg, the capital of Galicia, the crown province of the Austro-Hungarian Empire.

Buber's grandfather, Salomon Buber, was a famous Hebrew scholar. He was the editor of several books of the *Midrash*—Rabbinic interpretations of the Bible. Salomon Buber gave his grandson a good Hebrew education, teaching him Bible and Talmud. Buber's grandmother, Adele, taught him European languages. Thus Buber received an excellent early education both in Judaism and in European culture.

Buber's grandfather owned a large estate in Bukovina. On occasion, his father took him to the nearby village of Sadagora, the seat of a dynasty of Hasidic Rabbis. It was in Sadagora that Buber first observed the strong bond between the Rebbe and his followers and saw the Rebbe as "true leader" and his followers as "true community." These early experiences were to prove decisive for Buber's later development as an interpreter of Hasidism.

Buber's father managed the Bukovina estate. Martin often accompanied his father on walks around the farm. He was impressed by the direct, honest way his father treated the workers. Such a relationship between an employer and his workers was unusual. Buber was even more impressed by the way his father approached the animals, "almost as if they were people."⁴

Buber learned from his father that man could enter into a relationship with all living beings—with animals as well as with humans. As we have noted, Buber developed an unusual aptitude for deep experiences at a very early age; an additional sense, a mystical awareness. This special awareness enabled Buber to enter into deep relationships with people, with animals, even with a tree. This extraordinary sensitivity led him to his discovery of his relationship to God.

Buber's unusual aptitude for deep experiences is seen in his description of a relationship he formed with a horse, when he was eleven years old.

The Horse

Buber's autobiographical description of his experiences, as a boy, reveals his special sensitivity:

When I was eleven years of age, spending the summer on my grandparents estate, I used, as often as I could do it unobserved, to steal into the stable and gently stroke the neck of my darling, a broad dapple-gray horse. It was not a casual delight but a great, certainly friendly but also deeply stirring happening. If I am to explain it now, beginning from the still very fresh memory of my hand, I must say that what I experienced in touch with the animal was the Other, the immense Otherness of the Other, which, however, did not remain strange like the otherness of the ox and the ram, but rather let me draw near and touch it. When I stroked the mighty mane, sometimes marvelously smooth-combed, at other times just as astonishly wild, and felt the life beneath my hand, it was as though the element of vitality itself bordered on my skin, something that was not I, was certainly not akin to me, palpably the other, not just another, really the Other itself; and yet it let me approach, confided itself to me. . . . The horse, even when I had not begun by pouring oats for him into the manger, very gently raised his massive head, ears flicking, then snorted quickly, as a conspirator gives a signal meant to be recognizable only by his fellow conspirator; and I was approved.

But once—I do not know what came over the child, at any rate it was childlike enough—it struck me about the stroking, what fun it gave me, and suddenly I became conscious of my hand. The game went on as before, but something had changed. It was no longer the same thing. And the next day, after giving him a rich feed, when I stroked my friend's head he did not raise his head. A few years later, when I thought about the incident, I no longer supposed that the animal had noticed my defection. But at the time I had considered myself judged.[5]

What Buber discovered in this incident was that the ebb and flow of relationship can be present in contact with an animal. Buber found that when he gave himself unreservedly to the animal—when he was totally involved with the horse—he felt its vitality and he experienced the horse responding to him. But when he became conscious of his hand—when he became self-conscious—he felt that the magic of the relationship was gone. The interruption of unreserved contact—of reciprocity with the animal, Buber felt as a judgment, because he was no longer totally involved with the horse.

The key word, and the fundamental issue here, is that of reciprocity. A relationship, to be a real relationship, must involve reciprocity. It must be mutual, shared, felt and shown by both sides; for example, being united in reciprocal affection. The essence of the mystical attitude is reciprocity. The mystic feels that his relationship with nature, or with God, is mutual: the mystic feels grasped, seized, addressed by the "Other." The Other "says" something to him. In Buber's case, the "Other" was a horse, later he describes his relationship to a tree. But all relationships, Buber will discover, are included and consummated in the supreme relationship with God.

To get a clearer focus on the growth of Buber's mystical awareness, let us compare it to that of the modern Austrian composer Gustav Mahler, as expressed in his Third Symphony. The programmatic titles of each movement express a similar developing mystical awareness:

First Movement: Pan Awakes: Summer Marches In
Second Movement: What the Flowers in the Meadow Tell Me
Third Movement: What the Animals in the Forest Tell Me
Fourth Movement: What the Night Tells Me
Fifth Movement: What the Morning Bells Tell Me
Sixth Movement: What Love Tells Me

Mahler wrote that he could almost call the Sixth Movement, 'What God Tells Me' in the sense that God can only be comprehended as Love, the peak, the highest level from which one can view the world."[6]

In much the same way, Buber's mystical awareness was present in his relationships with animals and nature. A turning point in Buber's thinking will be reached with his new insights into human relationships. But the peak, the highest level—for Buber as it was for Mahler—will be the relationship with God. And the way to God, for Buber as for Mahler, was through love.

A Religious Crisis

Buber's pathway to God was not an easy one. He had to find God in his own way.

The way of the Jewish tradition did not at first appeal to him. Shortly after his *Bar Mitzvah*, he suffered a religious crisis. He found the rituals of Judaism no longer meaningful for him. At the age of fourteen, he ceased to put on *Tefillin* at morning prayers, thus breaking with a centuries-old Jewish tradition. He became alienated from Jewish traditions and rituals; he experienced a crisis of Jewish identity and personal identity.

What Buber was experiencing at this time was actually a crisis of meaning. He was seeking the meaning of man's place in the universe. And he became so frustrated in his quest for meaning that he contemplated suicide. Here is his description of this crisis:

> A necessity I could not understand swept over me: I had to try again and again to imagine the edge of space or its edgelessness, time with a beginning and an end or a time without beginning or end, and both were equally impossible, equally hopeless—yet there seemed to be only the choice between the one or the other absurdity. Under an irresistible compulsion I reeled from one to the other, at times so closely threatened with the danger of madness that I seriously thought of avoiding it by suicide.[7]

We see from this incident that philosophy, for Buber, was no mere academic exercise. Buber *had* to discover meaning in the universe; his very life was at stake. How did Buber resolve this crisis? Buber found the resolution of his philosophical dilemma in the work of the modern German philosopher, Immanuel Kant, who taught that space and time are forms of our perception of the world. Buber realized that through perception, we, in part, create the world we live in. He wrote:

> Being itself was beyond the reach alike of the finitude and the infinity of space and time, since it only appeared in space and time but did not itself enter into this appearance. At that time I began to gain an inkling of the existence of eternity as something quite different from the infinite, just as it is something quite different from the finite, and of the possibility of a connection between me, a man, and the eternal.[8]

Put simply, Buber realized that God, the eternal ultimate reality, is beyond the reach of our usual ways of knowing and our scientific categories—beyond space and time, beyond the finite and the infinite. Yet Buber believed that there was a connection between him and the Eternal. Thus Buber realized that another way of knowing (beside the scientific way) was necessary for man to become aware of his connection to the Eternal. This other way of knowing was to be found in deep mystical awareness. Accordingly, Buber strove to deepen his mystical awareness through a study of German and Jewish mysticism, especially in its modern Hasidic phase.

Study of Hasidism

When he was seventeen, Buber enrolled at the University of Vienna to study philosophy and the history of art. Through his philosophical and artistic studies, he became interested in the German mystics and their search for God. In 1904, Buber received his doctoral degree. The subject of his doctoral dissertation was a comparative study of one aspect of the thought of two German mystics, Nicolas of Cusa and Jakob Böhme.

Ever since Buber had left his grandfather's house at the age of fourteen, he had felt alienated from his Jewish roots. He describes his confusion at that time of his life:

> So long as I lived with [my grandfather], my roots were firm,

although many questions and doubts also jogged about in me. Soon after I left his house, the whirl of the age took me in. Until my twentieth year, and in small measure even beyond then, my spirit was in steady and multiple movement, in an alternation of tension and release, determined by manifold influences, taking ever new shape, but without center and without growing substance: it was really the 'Olam-ha-Tohu,' the 'World of Confusion,' the mythical dwelling place of the wandering souls.[9]

At first, Buber found refuge from this confusion in Zionism— the movement to restore the Jewish people to their homeland in Israel. Zionism meant for Buber his "renewed taking root in the community."[10] He became the editor of an important Zionist journal, *Der Jude*. One of the editors of this journal was a Roman Catholic woman named Paula Winkler. Buber's marriage to her when he was twenty-one helped him to find the inner unity he was seeking.

But he was seeking not only inner unity. The single thread that runs through the whole of Buber's life and thought is "his concern for unity: unity of the whole of Being, unity within an individual being, unity between individual beings."[11] Zionism had re-established Buber's connection with the Jewish people. But he was still searching for something spiritual within Judaism that would satisfy his quest for the unity of the whole of Being.

In his search for his spiritual Jewish roots, Buber renewed his study of Hebrew language and literature. In the book *Zevaat Ribesh* (the Testament of Rabbi Israel Baal-Shem), Buber came upon a statement of the Baal Shem Tov describing the intensity and depth of the daily renewal of the Hasid. Buber recognized this quality of intensity and return within himself. What was this statement of the Baal Shem Tov that opened the world of Hasidism? Buber writes dramatically of this event:

. . . the words flashed toward me. "He takes unto himself the quality of fervor. He arises from sleep with fervor, for he is hallowed and become another man and is worthy to create and is become like the Holy One, blessed be He, when He created the world." It was then that, overpowered in an instant, I experienced the Hasidic soul. The primally Jewish opened to me, flowering to newly conscious expression in the darkness of exile: man's being created in the image of God I grasped as deed, as becoming, as task.[12]

The concept of man as a partner with God in the never ending process of creation evoked Buber's own drive toward creativity. He recalled the image of the Rebbe and his followers from his childhood and the idea of the *Zaddik*—the perfected man. So moved was Buber by these ideas that at the age of twenty-six, he withdrew for five years from activities in the Zionist movement and immersed himself in the study of Hasidism. He spent these five years alone, in seclusion, studying the Hasidic tales and legends. He translated these tales and legends, introducing Hasidism to the modern world.

One of his earliest interpretations of Hasidism was an essay entitled "The Life of the Hasidim" (1908). In this selection, Buber describes *Hitlahavut*—Hasidic ecstasy:

> "*Hitlahavut* is 'the inflaming,' the ardor of ecstasy. . . . *Hitlahavut* unlocks the meaning of life. Without it even heaven has no meaning and no being. . . . Above nature and above time and above thought—thus is he called who is in ecstasy. . . . The man of ecstasy rules life, and no external happening that penetrates into his realm can disturb his inspiration."[13]

At this stage in his development, Buber emphasized mystic ecstasy—an overwhelming religious experience which took one out of the context of everyday life into a realm beyond nature and time, into another world, into contact with the "life beyond." But Buber discovered that this mystic withdrawal from the world to find God had its dangers. An external happening occurred that was to transform the emphasis of his thinking.

An Encounter
During World War I, when Buber was in his late thirties, a troubled young man came to see him, seeking his help. Buber had

spent the morning in religious ecstasy, trying to withdraw from the world to seek God. Now a young man sat before him, seeking his guidance. Evidently, Buber had already acquired a reputation as a wise man who could help people. Buber answered the questions this young man asked. He was courteous, polite and friendly. But he did not really try to understand the deeper feelings that were troubling his visitor.

Shortly after this visit, Buber learned that the young man had died at the front "out of a despair that did not oppose his own death."[14] Buber sadly realized that he had not reached this man. He had not really entered into a relationship with him.

This tragic event led Buber to revise his ideas about the way to reach God. He now believed that it was not necessary to withdraw from the world in ecstasy to attain to an experience of the Divine. On the contrary! Buber now viewed the message of Hasidism in a different way: that "God can be beheld in each thing and reached through each pure deed."[15] Buber's emphasis on Hasidic ecstasy was replaced by the concept of the hallowing of the everyday which is the essence of Hasidism. We meet God, Buber now taught, *through* our relationships with our fellow human beings, not by withdrawing from them.

This became the most important teaching of Martin Buber: the relationship of "I" and "Thou."

I and Thou

I and Thou was Buber's most important book and his most significant teaching. The book was first published in 1923, when Buber was forty-five.

In this book, Buber draws a contrast between two types of relationships and two types of knowing: "I—It" and "I—Thou."

Consider, for example, two teachers. One teacher is not really interested in his students as human beings. They are merely numbers for him, inseparable from the marks he records in his gradebook. The relationship of this teacher to his students is an "I—It" relationship.

Another teacher, by contrast, is interested in his students as persons. He is concerned about their personal growth as individuals. This teacher—and Buber himself as a Professor at the Hebrew University is said to have done this—responds to the questions of each student by actually walking over to the student's desk and looking directly into his eyes. This teacher seeks an "I—Thou" relationship with his students. Such a relationship would be mutual, direct, and exclusive; involving the whole being of both teacher and student. Both teacher and student would be totally absorbed in the "encounter."

Clearly, "I—Thou" relationships with other persons cannot last forever. People have different moods. People change. When two people marry, for example, they may be deeply in love. Their relationship may be an "I—Thou" relationship. But, like Buber's parents, their love for one another may not last. They may lose their love for one another. Their marriage may end in divorce. But even happily married people cannot sustain an "I—Thou" relationship all the time. Eventually, as Buber says, every "Thou" *except one*, must become an "it."

The exception, Buber claimed, was God, who is the eternal Thou. God is the Supreme Being, the eternal Thou who can never become an "It." In *I and Thou*, Buber says concerning God: " . . . God is the Being that is directly, most nearly, and lastingly over against us, that may properly only be addressed, not expressed."[16]

Buber's idea of God in *I and Thou* is very different from the concept of God of the early Jewish mystics.

To the "Merkabah" mystics, God was far away, remote, in heaven.

To Buber, in *I and Thou*, God is an eternal companion, near and close, to be talked to and discovered on earth.

Notice that Buber says that God can only be talked to, addressed, and not talked about or expressed. Buber believed that he had discovered another way of knowing besides the scientific way. In science, we describe our knowledge of something by talking about it. In the spiritual life, by contrast, Buber maintained that we can know God only by entering into a relationship with

Him, just as we can know other people only by forming relationships with them. But the knowledge of God is indescribable, ineffable: God can only be addressed, not expressed.

Although the knowledge of persons can be expressed, there is one human relationship that is ineffable: love. Love creates an ineffable unity between people. And ultimately, it is love of the world, Buber believes, that opens the way to God. Buber's quest for unity culminates in love. As Buber wrote: "Meet the world with the fullness of your being and you shall meet God. If you wish to believe, love."[17]

Rav Kook's Spiritual Journey

Rabbi Abraham Isaac Kook's personal goal was a life of holiness—a spiritual life comparable to a journey from darkness into light. His concept of this life of holiness was linked to the pulsating vitality of the world and the infinite life of God. For Kook, the mystical experience united the individual with humanity, with the universe and with God. The main image Rav Kook used to describe his personal religious experiences was that of *light*. Kook viewed his mystical experiences as a series of illuminations that came to him from God. It is, therefore, no coincidence that three of his works include the term "lights": *Lights*[18]—a collection of essays, *The Lights of Penitence*[19] and *The Lights of Holiness*.[20]

How can an individual experience these Divine lights, these illuminations from God? Like Martin Buber, Rav Kook was a seeker after unity. He sought the type of spiritual perception which would "embrace everything in togetherness."[21] Like Buber, he affirmed the unifying power of love: love of all creation, love for mankind, love for the Jewish people and the highest of all loves—for God.[22] But Rav Kook's scope is wider than Buber's; his quest is not only for a feeling of unity through inner personal awareness but also for a cosmic vision of *universality*. It is the principle of universality—liberation from one's private concerns, freeing one to experience belonging to the universe, to all existence—that was the spiritual "light" sought by Rav Kook. The following words of Kook are enlightening for all who seek in mysticism a way of widening their horizons:

> A person must liberate himself from confinement within his private
> concerns. This pervades his whole being so that all his thoughts focus
> on his own destiny. It reduces him to the worst kind of smallness, and
> brings upon him endless physical and spiritual distress. It is necessary
> to raise a person's thought and will and his basic preoccupations to-
> ward universality, to the inclusion of all, to the whole world, to man,
> to the Jewish people, to all existence. This will result in establishing
> even his private self on a proper basis.
>
> The firmer a person's vision of universality, the greater the joy he
> will experience, and the more he will merit the grace of divine illumi-
> nation. The reality of God's providence is discernible when the world
> is seen in its totality.[23]

Hachala—the Hebrew word for inclusion—represents the aim of
Rav Kook's spiritual vision. A cell is included within an organ, an
organ within a body, the body within the total person, the person
within humanity, humanity within the cosmos, the cosmos within
God—this series of ever-widening, concentric circles, each more
inclusive than the preceding, informs Rav Kook's vision of the
world.

No partial perspective could satisfy Rav Kook. What he sought,
he expressed lyrically in these poetic words:

> *Expanses, expanses*
> *Expanses divine, my soul doth crave.*
> *Enclose me not in cages, of matter or mind.*
> *Through heavenly vastness my soul doth soar . . .* [24]

Rav Kook's quest to transcend the everyday world through
mysticism speaks to all who find the pettiness of everyday life con-
fining and restricting. Nevertheless, Rav Kook did not ignore
everyday concerns in his own life. On the contrary! As we look
back upon his life, and his eventual calling to the position of
Ashkenazic Chief Rabbi of Israel, we shall see a fascinating syn-
thesis of the spiritual and the secular, expressed most dramatically

in his espousal of the cause of the non-religious pioneers in Eretz Yisrael.

From the Heder to the Holy Land

Abraham Isaac Kook was born in the year 1865, in the little Jewish community of Grieve, a shtetl in northwestern Russia.[25] At an early age, Kook was immersed in Torah study and the sea of the Talmud. His first experiences in Judaism were of the limited, restricted atmosphere of the *Heder*—the traditional school of the Jewish ghetto.

Just as Rav Kook was to transcend narrowness of all kinds in the universality of his mysticism, so was he, by the age of nine, already thought of as an *illuy* (child prodigy) and was no longer required to attend the *Heder*. Instead, a corner of the ancient synagogue was designated for him and he was allowed to study there on his own as a *matmid*—an unusually diligent student.

At the age of fifteen, Abraham Isaac was described as "a handsome youth, of middle height, pale face and large bright glowing brown eyes."[26] It was at this age that his parents decided to send him to the small town of Lutzin, to study there in the old *Beth Hamidrash* (house of study). The simple faith and intense piety of the young student of Lutzin reflected the culture of the masses of Russian Jewry, who were still unaffected by the new intellectual and social currents of the modern world.

After a few years, Abraham Isaac left the small town of Lutzin and travelled to Smargon, a large and teeming metropolis. There he encountered the *Maskilim*, or "enlightened ones," who were immersed in secular notions such as Darwin's theory of evolution and Nietzsche's philosophy of the Superman. It does not appear that Abraham Isaac's faith was shaken by these new currents of thought. As a matter of fact, we shall see that in the development of his thought, Rav Kook views evolution as a confirmation of his own dynamic view of the universe.

More influential than the *Maskilim* on Kook's thinking was the effect of Rabbi Yisrael Salanter and the *mussar* movement. It was during his stay in Smargon that Abraham Isaac joined this move-

ment. As the term *mussar* (moral discipline) indicated, this movement emphasized the ideal of personal perfection through ceaseless
self-examination. Man's goal, according to the *mussar* movement,
was spiritual perfection: a pious state of mind to be achieved
through a vigorous process of self-discipline in which fear,
jealousy, anger, greed and egotism were to be overcome and
various ethical virtues were to be acquired. The quest for moral
and spiritual perfection—which Kook first learned from the
mussar movement—was to play a significant role in his mystical
philosophy.

From Smargon, the young scholar went to the famous academy
of Volozhin, which was then under the leadership of the
"Netsiv," Rabbi Naphtali Zvi Y'huda Berlin. At this famous
Yeshivah and center of Talmudic learning, Kook's colleagues and
teachers were impressed not only by his phenomenal memory and
diligence in study but also by his devotion and piety. Commented
a former roommate of Kook: "Every prayer that was uttered by
Abraham Isaac was thoroughly soaked with tears."[27] Here were
the first stirrings of that powerful religious consciousness that was
to find expression in his spiritual diaries.

During his student years at Volozhin, Abraham Isaac became
engaged to the daughter of Rabbi Eliyahu David Rabinowitz-
Tomin, the Rabbi of Ponivesh. After he married, he moved to the
house of his father-in-law, where he continued to pursue his
Talmudic studies. At that time and place in Jewish history, the
customary marriage arrangements called for the son-in-law to
board with the parents of his wife for a number of years. Freed
from the need for providing for his family, the young husband
could devote himself completely during these years to Torah and
Talmud study. We can picture the young scholar at that time, sitting at a desk studying the holy books with his *tallis* (prayer shawl)
and *tefillin* (prayer phylacteries) on, feeling that these holy objects
would inspire him with the proper mood of consecration to God's
Word. Already, at this young age, we see the growth of piety as a
state of mind—the development of a uniquely religious consciousness—in the person of Abraham Isaac Kook.

Ideally, Abraham Isaac would have liked to devote his entire life to his yearning for God through the development of his mystical consciousness. The time came, however, when Abraham had to decide on a career. His father-in-law had suggested the Rabbinate. In order to achieve the financial independence necessary to pursue his devotional goals, Abraham Isaac engaged in various commercial enterprises. Unfortunately, his investments failed. Abraham Isaac slowly became reconciled to the fact that his life would not only contain the unrestricted and free soarings of his mystical mind but also the restricted and limited concerns of a Rabbi in a small town.

It was during this period of uncertainty regarding his future vocation that Abraham Isaac met Rabbi Israel Meir of Radin, known as the *Chofetz Chayim*. Rabbi Meir's book of the same name deals with the evils of *Loshen Hora*—speaking evil of one's fellow man. The theme embodied in the title of this book is that one who seeks life ("Chofetz Chayim"), i.e., the good life, should shun slander, gossip and evil talk of all kinds. Befriended by this saintly man and nurtured by his piety, Abraham Isaac's religious consciousness matured. The *Chofetz Chayim* convinced Abraham of the necessity for spiritual leadership in an age beset with spiritual confusion. Persuaded by Rabbi Israel Meir, Kook began his practical Rabbinate by accepting a call to be the Rabbi of the small town of Zoimel. During his six years in Zoimel, in addition to his pastoral duties, Rabbi Kook came under the influence of the Kabbalist, Rabbi Solomon Eliashev of Shavell. Studying the Lurianic Kabbalah with him, Rav Kook's soul was receiving further preparations for the mystical illuminations that would stir his consciousness.

At the age of thirty, Kook became the Rabbi of the comparatively larger city of Boisk, in Lithuania. At Boisk (1895-1904), Rabbi Kook's spiritual stature grew. Through his sermons and writings, he became known as an outstanding ideologist for Orthodox Jewry. In particular, he became Orthodoxy's chief spokesman for Zionism. Kook saw Jewish nationalism or Zionism—the movement to reestablish the Jewish

homeland in Israel—as the manifestation of a Divine aspect in the
soul of the Jew. Zionist nationalism, for Kook, was not in conflict
with universalism, because it is through loyalty to his people that
the Jew can contribute most to humanity. Thus for Kook, Jewish
nationalism possesses a holy dimension: it is a religious obligation
because of the inner mystical bond between the Jewish people and
the Holy Land.

In accordance with his Zionist ideology, Kook longed to settle
permanently in the Holy Land—the place where he felt that the
soul of the Jew regains its roots and its vital force. Thus, he accepted the call to be the Rabbi of the city of Jaffa in Israel in 1904.
Abraham Isaac Kook's spiritual journey, thus far, had taken him
from the Heder to the Holy Land.

The Spiritual in the Secular

The spiritual and the secular are usually seen as two distinct
realms. "Secular" (from the Latin *saeculum*—world) denotes
worldly, mundane matters—generally pertaining to the week-day.
Spiritual or sacred matters are generally confined to Sabbaths and
other holy days—times and places set apart for religious devotion.
To Rav Kook, the "spiritual" and the "secular" did not constitute
a dichotomy: they were not two separate realms. In fact, as his
thought developed, Rav Kook saw no dichotomies or separations
in the world. Rather, he perceived harmony and unity: an all-
embracing perspective. As we follow Rav Kook's life in Israel as
Rabbi of Jaffa (1904-1919) and as Chief Rabbi of Israel in
Jerusalem (1919-1935), we shall see that the unifying theme of his
Rabbinate was his uncanny mystical ability to sense the spiritual in
the secular; or to put it differently, to see the secular or worldly as
a vehicle for the spirit.

In order to be able to perceive the spiritual in the secular, Rav
Kook had to be a mystic of extraordinary spiritual sensitivity. He
reached this degree of spiritual illumination in Israel. It was during
his stay in Jaffa that Rav Kook began to have exalted and ineffable
mystical illuminations. In these mystical illuminations, he felt the
"glow of the Holy Spirit" bursting forth, the "sweetness and light

of holiness" that can be discovered by those who truly seek God. The unique challenge that Rav Kook responded to was to find the spiritual dimension, not only in mystical experience, but also in the secular world. As he became well known as the brilliant Rabbi of Jaffa, many individuals turned to him for advice. A major problem he was asked to resolve was the growing alienation between pious parents and their free-thinking children.[28] Here the uniqueness of Rav Kook's approach came into play. Rather than casting aspersions on the free-thinking youth for their disaffection from Orthodoxy, Rav Kook pointed out that the heresies of the present often derive from idealistic motives; the search for truth and secular learning that motivated these young people to break with tradition were in themselves noble sentiments. It was Rav Kook's hope that in the end, through their devotion to Jewish nationalism, these secular young people would return to their ancestral faith.

Elevated to Ashkenazic Chief Rabbi of Israel in Jerusalem (1919-1935), Rav Kook's aim was also to bridge the gap between the traditionalists of the "old Yishuv" and the new secular-minded immigrants who entered the Holy Land after the Balfour Declaration of 1917—in which Britain pledged her support of the Zionist hope for the establishment of a Jewish national home. Convinced that the time for the Messianic redemption of the Jewish people was imminent, Rav Kook perceived a spiritual element in the secularism of the new immigrants. Who actually were these new immigrants and how vast were their differences with the "old Yishuv"?

From 1919 to 1935, the Jewish population in Israel grew from 90,000 to about 400,000. Prior to the twentieth century, Jewish life in Israel had been dominated by the "Old Yishuv"—those who had come to Israel to sanctify God through a life of prayer and study and to be buried in the holy soil of Eretz Yisrael.

With the advent of the twentieth century and especially after the Balfour Declaration, new "secular" immigrants entered Israel. These were young people motivated by secular ideals such as the fervor of Jewish nationalism or Russian socialism; they were indif-

ferent to religion and generally agnostic or atheistic. It was a for-
midable task Rav Kook set himself to unite these two diverse
worlds.

It is readily understandable that Rav Kook's defense of the
"godless" *halutzim*—the new secular Israeli pioneers—would
engender the bitter hostility of the extreme Orthodox element in
Jerusalem. How, in the face of this hostility, did Kook, an Orthodox Rabbi, defend his stance in sympathy with the *halutzim?*

Kook defended his view both by an historical analogy and a
philosophical observation on the "value" of atheism.

First, the historical analogy: Kook pointed out that in ancient
Israel, the Holy of Holies was the most sacred part of the Temple.
So great was its holiness that only the High Priest could enter
it—and he could only do so on the Day of Atonement and after he
had undergone a complex ritual of purification. But the situation
was different when the Temple was being built and the Holy of
Holies was being constructed. At that time, the artisans and
assistants were allowed to enter with their tools, in their working
clothes and without preliminary purification. By the same token,
Kook claimed, the Holy Land is in the process of being built. The
halutzim, the working men, are like the ancient artisans: they are
building the Holy of Holies. Therefore, they cannot be judged by
traditional standards of piety. "Let them work," counselled Rav
Kook. "When the Holy Land is built up, then," Rav Kook claimed, "we can re-introduce these traditional standards of piety."[29]
Rav Kook's belief that the historical period he was entering was
the beginning of the Messianic redemption was a significant factor
in his espousal of the cause of the "godless" *halutzim*: he considered it the atheism which is due to arise prior to the messianic
liberation.

Philosophically, too, Rav Kook was unique among religious
leaders in seeing value in atheism. Kook wrote:

> Atheism has a temporary legitimacy, for it is needed to purge away
> the aberrations that attached themselves to religious faith because of a
> deficiency in perception and in the divine service. This is its sole func-

tion in existence—to remove the *particular* images from the speculations concerning Him who is the *essence* of all life and the source of all
thought.[30]

Rav Kook firmly believed that we cannot know the essence of
God. He maintained that we can only know and encounter God's
"lights": His effects in the world, His manifestations, His ideals,
His attributes. The atheist, according to Kook, therefore performs
a valuable service in exposing as idolatry the claims of those who
pretend to know the essence of God.

Thus, Rav Kook's thoughts about God were continuous with
the insight that informs both the Jewish mystical and philosophical
tradition. This is especially evident in the unknowability of the
Divine essence—(which was also a dominant theme in Moses
Maimonides' philosophy); that no positive statement can be made
about the essence of God, about what God really is—we can only
know God's attributes.

Yet Rav Kook was just as emphatic in his claim that though we
cannot know *what* God is, we do know *that* God is: we do know
that there is an ineffable source of the universe and an essence of all
life. Rav Kook was not content merely to know this conceptually.
Like all true mystics, he sought to experience the light and love of
God. He wrote: "I thirst for truth, not concepts of truth."[31] And
it is said that towards the end of his life, when a visitor to his home
asked him to come to the synagogue to take part in the evening
service, Rav Kook replied, "I can't go with you. I am all afire with
the love of God. If I should go now to the synagogue I might be
completely consumed. Let us rather go out for a walk that I might
cool off."[32]

Indicative of the saintliness of Rav Kook was his capacity to
maintain his steadfast faith in God when he was dying of cancer,
to which he finally succumbed on the 3rd of Elul, 1935. Once
when he was in the throes of the agony of this dreaded disease, he
was said to have exclaimed: "No man knows how grateful he
should be for the sufferings that come to him, since through them
he can attain the highest levels of the love of God."[33]

Rav Kook's courage to affirm the Rabbinic concept of *Yissurim Shel Ahavah* (chastisements of God's love) echoes the spiritual fortitude of the early Jewish mystic, Rabbi Akiba, who affirmed God's love and unity as his flesh was being combed with iron during his martyr's death at the hands of the Romans. The saintliness of men like Rabbi Akiba and Rav Kook can be attributed to a higher mystical power and insight—actualized in them, but only latent in others.

Just as we listen to the works of a great composer to deepen our musical sensitivity, so we contemplate the words and thoughts of Jewish mystical artists of the soul such as Rav Kook to understand Jewish mysticism. In this vein, let us now contemplate some of the lofty and inspired thoughts of Rabbi Abraham Isaac Kook, to see how he elevated his soul to such a degree of saintliness.

The Mystic Path: From Fragmentation to Unity

All of us seek inner peace. What prevents us from finding inner peace is that our souls are beset with conflict. Our feelings may conflict with our thoughts; our drives may be at war with our ideals: we are fragmented into parts. A part of us may long for aesthetic contemplation; another part of us may yearn for love; still another part of us may wish to escape from our finite predicament. Rav Kook was not immune from such an inner struggle. But such an "inner battle" signified for him the prelude to a mystical experience of psychic unity. Thus, Rav Kook wrote:

> How great is my inner battle!
> My heart is filled with yearning,
> spiritual, multi-directional,
> I beg for sweetness, divine, to
> permeate me . . . [34]

In another context, Rav Kook interpreted the fundamental Jewish concept of *Teshuvah* or penitence as the return to perfection in God, arising out of deliverance from the "world of fragmentation" and immersion into the mystical "world of unity":

When a person sins he has entered the world of fragmentation, and then every particular being stands by itself, and evil is evil in and of itself, and it is evil and destructive. When he repents out of love there at once shines on him the light from the world of unity, where everything is integrated into one whole, and in the context of the whole there is no evil at all.[35]

The mystical experience of unity is thus a goal open to all who "repent out of love."

How did Rav Kook envisage the mystical "world of unity"? He conceived of it, idealistically, as held together by one all-embracing Divine thought. In his mystic vision of unity, Rav Kook wrote:

We see the Supreme Thought, the Thought which embraces all things, the Thought which contains the power and the fullness of the whole. We see that all the great rivers flow from it, and streams issue from the rivers, and brooks from the streams, and the brooks divide into many channels and the channels divide into many thousands, indeed an infinity of little canals, which pour forth the bounty of will, life and thought.[36]

This vision of the entire universe as the product of the thought of a Supreme Mind is not merely an imaginative conception. It is a contemporary world view maintained by scientists who espouse an "organic" or holistic view of the universe rather than a "mechanistic" or materialistic world-view (according to which the universe is a product of the random movements of atoms and molecules). Illustrative of the "organic" viewpoint is the following statement of the British scientist Sir James Jean:

Today there is a wide measure of agreement, which on the physical side of science approaches almost to unanimity, that the stream of knowledge is heading toward a non-mechanical reality; *the universe begins to look more like a great thought than like a great machine.* Mind no longer appears as an accidental intruder into the realm of matter; we are beginning to suspect that we ought rather to hail it as the creator and governor of the realm of matter—not of course our individual minds, but the mind in which the atoms out of which our individual minds have grown exist as thoughts.[37]

In addition to the testimony of Sir James Jean, the physicist Fritjof Capra, in his book *The Tao of Physics*, cites as one of the fundamental parallels between modern physics and Eastern mysticism the concept of the unity of the universe: "The basic oneness of the universe is not only the central characteristic of the mystical experience, but is also one of the most important revelations of modern physics."[38] Thus in his quest to transcend the fragmentation of our ordinary existence in which we categorize inner and outer reality into separate parts, and in his mystical intuition of the unity of the universe, Rav Kook was at one not only with other mystics who sought inner and cosmic unity but also with scientists seeking a holistic, organic and unified concept of ultimate reality.

The Mystical Experience

Rav Kook, we have noted, was a literary mystic: he described the actual content of his mystical experiences. Among the images he used to describe his experiences were those of sound and of light. Of the sounds he heard from a higher spiritual realm, he wrote:

> Waves from the higher realm act on our souls ceaselessly. The stirrings of our inner spiritual sensibilities are the result of the sounds released by the violin of our souls, as it listens to the echo of the sound emanating from the divine realm.[39]

Just as a musical composer has a unique consciousness of sound, so too does the mystic. There is an aesthetic realm of sound, and there is also a spiritual dimension whose voice a gifted mystic like Rav Kook can hear. Since the "song of Rav Kook's soul" was an ongoing spiritual melody, he was able to listen to the transcendent realm, to hear the voice of God.

In a similar manner, Rav Kook used the image of waves of light to describe his mystical experience:

The spiritual waves stirring the individual and the world derive from the inner endeavor of all things to conform to the inflow of the light of the *En Sof.*

In one moment there is a flash of light, and life is enhanced as the will is filled with delight in the envisioned conformity to the absolute good in the light of the *En Sof.* A great satisfaction moves through all the avenues of life and of all existence.[40]

For Rav Kook, in accord with the Jewish mystical tradition, the *En Sof*—the infinite essence of God—is unknowable. Finite man is incapable of knowing the infinite, unlimited essence of God. But Rav Kook believed that we *can* know and we *can* experience—as he did—the spiritual light emanating from the *En Sof.* Rav Kook's mystical experience was of God's lights: His ideals, His attributes, His effects. The mystical experience of Rav Kook was thus not a *unio mystica*—a mystical union with God (a type of experience virtually absent from the Jewish mystical tradition). It was rather one of *Devekut:* cleaving to God's lights, to the Divine attributes.

But even this flash of Divine light is intermittent. When it passes, the mystic feels the spiritual depression known as "the dark night of the soul." Having tasted, having glimpsed a ray of the Divine light—and then having the glow abate—is a devastating experience. Here is Rav Kook's description of his own "dark night of the soul"—a Jewish depiction of the ebb and flow of the mystical consciousness:

Then there at once settles on us the realization how dark and deficient everything is in comparison with the En Sof, what endless abysses separate the Creator from the creature, and how impossible is this desire for conformity. And everything seems dry and empty.

But out of this very depression over the nothingness of everything, and that the source of all is everything, and the mighty higher reality of the divine light, its affirmation and splendor, fills all the vital parts of body and soul. . . . Man then rises, his soul's confidence and the eternal significance of his life are again strengthened. He rises toward the heights until he feels crushed and desperate, but his spirit is at once renewed, and again becomes luminous. It "is a forward and backward movement, like the appearance of a flash of lightning" (Ezekiel 1:14).[41]

R'tzo V'shuv—running and returning, forward and backward—this is the movement of the mystical consciousness. Ebb and flow, darkness and light, distance and nearness, spiritual depression and elation—these are the alternating currents, the feelings of the mystic. There is nothing to compare with the ineffable joy of the mystic as he experiences the Divine light, the flash of God's nearness. But this experience is transitory; it quickly passes. As the mystic returns to "ordinary consciousness," he recognizes the deep chasm separating the mundane world from the spiritual world—the world for which his soul longs. The awareness of this gulf fills the mystic with a feeling of depression—a sadness that he begins to overcome only when he expresses his longing for God in the words of prayer.

Prayer: The Yearning for God

Rav Kook did not find Darwin's theory of evolution threatening to Judaism. On the contrary, he believed that of all the concepts of modern science, Darwin's theory came closest to the spirit of Jewish mysticism. As far as the seeming incompatibility between Darwin's theory and the story of creation in Genesis was concerned, Kook maintained that a symbolic rather than a literal interpretation of the creation story removes the conflict. For example, if each "day" of creation is understood to be symbolic of billions of years, much of the alleged conflict between Genesis and science is dissipated.

What Rav Kook appreciated in Darwin's theory of evolution was the view of reality he believed it gave rise to: a concept of the propelling force in the world as vital, forward-moving and dynamic. Rav Kook also viewed sympathetically the concept of creative evolution put forward by the modern French Jewish philosopher, Henri Bergson. Bergson saw the essence of reality as an *elan vital*—a vital force, a dynamic creative process, albeit not necessarily a purposive flow.

Therefore, unlike Darwin—who saw the blind struggle for survival as the driving force of evolution, and unlike Bergson—who saw the motive power as a creative but purposeless vital force, Rav Kook maintained that the moving force behind evolution was the yearning of every existent being for a return to its source, a return to God.

Prayer for Rav Kook, is precisely that aspiration of every creature for the perfection that can only be attained by returning to the Source of All—to Almighty God. Rav Kook's description of prayer is both poetic and powerful:

> Prayer is the ideal of all worlds. All of being aspires toward the source of its life; every flower and every blade of grass, every grain of sand and clod of earth; the things which throb visibly with life and those in which life is concealed; the smallest beings of creation and the largest, the angels and the holy seraphs of heaven, all the particularity of being and all its universality—everything longs and aspires, craves and yearns for the perfection of its high, holy, pure and mighty Source.[42]

Prayer, for Rav Kook, was thus not merely a formal repetition of hallowed words. Nor was it merely a petition to God to satisfy our needs. Prayer was man's craving for growth toward perfection, toward spirituality. Prayer for Rav Kook was also a cosmic phenomenon: the plants pray, the flowers sing to God, all life is prayer, all breath is a praise of God. Accordingly, Rav Kook wrote: "Prayer is an absolute necessity for us and *for the whole world*, also the most sacred kind of joy. . . . "[43]

Prayer to Rav Kook is the song of the soul of all existence. He saw the entire cosmos as a symphony to God.

Rav Kook's philosophy of prayer embodies in miniature his entire world view: his powerful and poignant mystic vision of the entire universe ceaselessly moving in love toward its ultimate Source and Creator—God.

Buber and Kook

Both Martin Buber and Rav Kook express the themes of unity,

love and devotion to God. But whereas Buber's base is one of
religious humanism, moving from man's inner feeling and his love
for his fellow human being toward love of the Eternal
Thou—God, Rav Kook's mysticism is wider and more universal
in scope, culminating in his lofty vision of the entire cosmos as a
prayer to God, its Creator.

Our horizons are widened, and our spirits deepened by these
two thinkers. Their noble thoughts move us in the direction of
spirituality: inwardly, to seek spiritual strength within ourselves;
outwardly, to search for human dignity and the soul of our fellow
human beings; and to the cosmos,.to "see the world in a grain of
sand";[44] and to see the world as a surging, streaming movement
toward fulfillment and perfection in God.

How can we relate these transcendent visions of the Divine to
our own concrete lives? Are there contemporary options open to
modern Jews which will fulfill their longings for a wider, all-
embracing Judaism?

To answer these questions, we shall enter into dialogue with a
mystically oriented American Rabbi who has a unique concept of
spirituality, emphasizing an aspect of God in Judaism which was
also stressed by Rav Kook. This is the Divine attribute expressed
in the vital force or creative process through which God—the eternal creative source of all—lures the world toward its final consum-
mation in Him. It is known in the Siddur, the Jewish prayer book,
as *Chei Ha-Olamim*: the Life of all Worlds.

The Legitimacy of Contemporary Options

Gershom Scholem, professor at the Hebrew University and the
world's leading authority on Jewish mysticism, maintains that the
Jew is now living in a time of transition, when he must be open to
new forms and trends. The following statement of Scholem argues
for the realization that Judaism cannot be frozen into any one
category and that many forms of Judaism, including contemporary
mystical trends, are legitimate and no less Jewish because of their
modernity and newness:

> There is no way of telling *a priori* what beliefs are possible or impos-

sible within the framework of Judaism. Certainly no serious historian would accept the specious argument that the criteria of Jewish belief were clear and evident until the kabbalah beclouded and confused the minds. The Jewishness in the religiosity of any particular period is not measured by dogmatic criteria that are unrelated to actual historical circumstances, but solely by what sincere Jews do, in fact, believe, or—at least—consider to be legitimate possibilities.[45]

It is an openness to new forms of Judaism and a willingness not to freeze Judaism into any *a priori* framework that is the attitude necessary to appreciate the contemporary options open to Jews in search of the mysticism they cannot find in the "organized Jewish religion" of our time; the spirituality they do not discover within the framework of the contemporary American "establishment" synagogue.

In order to discover what contemporary options are open to the Jewish seeker who is dissatisfied with conventional Jewish worship, I visited with Rabbi Everett Gendler. Unlike many other Rabbis whose theological views are firm and fixed, Rabbi Gendler's view exemplifies an open and experimental attitude toward Jewish belief and practice. Who is Everett Gendler? What is his background? And what contemporary options does he envision for the Jew of today in search of spirituality?

Contemporary Options

I first met Everett Gendler when I was a Rabbinical student at the Jewish Theological Seminary. His spirituality immediately impressed me. Casual in dress, tall and thin in appearance, he radiated an aura of refinement. His concerns were matters of depth; prayer, nature, peace. He was exceedingly perceptive and articulate in the way he expressed these concerns. Most important of all, he conveyed the fact that he was a man of the spirit, in search of a more articulate Jewish spirituality.

What is Everett's background? He was born in Chariton, Iowa and lived there until the age of eleven. Chariton is a small town surrounded by open country, where, Gendler has said, "nature was omnipresent."[46] Here he first became aware of the beauties of nature. Here were the first stirrings of that love of nature which was to play such an important part in his spirituality.

At the age of eleven, he moved to Des Moines, where he became acquainted with the Quakers. They "spoke to his condition." What he found most attractive about the Quakers was "their reflective silence in worship, their considerate gentleness and their religious involvement in social issues."[47]

One could say that Everett, a gentle individual himself, injects a Quaker-like atmosphere into Judaism.

However, it was not until after he was ordained as a Rabbi at the Jewish Theological Seminary and spent a period of time serving a congregation in the valley of Mexico that "nature as such"[48] came more fully to his awareness.

On my recent visit to his home, amidst the beauty of the lovely New England country town of Andover, Massachusetts, Everett Gendler emphasized a new awareness of "nature elements in Jewish worship" as a contemporary spiritual option open to the modern Jew, reminding us of the nature mysticism of Rabbi Nachman of Bratslav. What does Gendler mean by "nature elements in Jewish worship"? And how can the awareness of these elements become a contemporary spiritual option?

Gendler maintains that Judaism has allowed itself to become so historically oriented that ties with the natural world have been broken, and that therefore the natural world has ceased to be a source of wonder to the Jew. "To be sure," Gendler indicates, "the break with paganism was vitally necessary for the development of Judaism. But the break can go too far," he contends. "It can become a chasm, an unbridgeable gap. We are at a stage now where we must begin to redress the balance by renewing our contact with nature. And furthermore, there originally were nature elements in Judaism, which we must revive."[49] What are some of these nature elements that Gendler would re-introduce into Jewish worship?

The most significant nature element in Jewish worship, according to Gendler, was the "faithfulness of the folk to the rhythms of the moon throughout the ages."[50] He points out that in the

Biblical period, *Rosh Hodesh* (New Moon) was a holy day comparable to the Sabbath. Commerce was prohibited (Amos 8:5), visits to men of God were customary and the New Moon offerings prescribed in Numbers (28:9-15) exceeded those prescribed for Sabbaths.

Why then has the observance of *Rosh Hodesh* as a holy day diminished in importance since Biblical times? It seems likely, Gendler notes, that "the prevailing rabbinic attitude toward the moon was hostile, and that in so far as *Rosh Hodesh* survived at all, it was due to the loyalty of the folk, not the representatives of the severely antipagan official tradition."[51]

Why does Gendler place so much emphasis on this folk feeling for the moon? He sees the moon as a symbol of our connection with the rhythms of the cosmos. Whereas the sun is always the same, the moon waxes, wanes, and disappears. The moon is thus symbolic of the human condition: human life is subject to the universal laws of birth, becoming, and death. It is precisely this connection with the cosmic rhythms of the universe that Gendler seeks to renew. He identifies this experience as a connection with the Divine, as he understands it. Gendler has written:

> No longer attuned to the cosmic rhythms about him, increasingly entombed by the contrived, manmade elements of his environment, he neither knows himself as microcosm nor has any felt, enlivening connection with *Chei Ha-olamim*, the life of the Universe (a term for the Divine which twice occurs in the traditional morning service).[52]

I asked Everett to explain his conception of God as the "Life of the Universe," which he based on the Hebrew phrase in the prayer book: *Chei Ha-olamim*. Everett replied that to him, God is "the pulse, the beat, the rhythm, the spout, the fountain of the universe."[53] He sees the presence of God in the process of growth: in helping food grow, or in watching the growth of a child into an adult. Unlike modern man, ancient man was constantly in contact with *Chei Ha-olamim*. To renew our contact with nature, Gendler adovcates services out of doors (whenever possible) in which "periods of silence and meditation on trees and shrubs"[54] are part of the worship. He also suggests a renewal of the ceremony of *Kiddush hal'vanah* (the sanctification of the waxing moon), "an out-of-door ceremony dating from Talmudic times which requires visual contact with the moon between the third and fifteenth days of the lunar month, and which also includes dancing before the moon"[55]; an extended service for *Rosh Hodesh*, the New Moon. And he recommends walking among grass and trees from earliest spring to latest autumn, seeing these aspects of nature as eloquent testimonials to the power of *Chei Ha-olamim*, the Life of the Universe, and chanting a prayer such as the following:

> *Master of the Universe,*
> *grant me the ability to be alone;*
> *may it be my custom to go outdoors each day*
> *among the trees and grass,*
> *among all growing things,*
> *and there may I be alone,*
> *and enter into prayer,*
> *to talk with the One that I belong to.*"[56]

Here is the essence of mystical awareness: a personal experience binding one to the universe, the feeling of the individual that he or she belongs somewhere—to the cosmos or to the Cosmic One.

In this connection, I asked Everett if his conception of God as the "Life of the Universe" connoted Someone as well as Something. Everett said that he does have a sense of God as a personal Being, but in a very subtle sense. God, he said, is somehow present amid—in—all things. Everett indicated that there was a time when he found the notion of a personal God to be difficult for him. More and more, however, the God of Nature has taken on for him "a personal aspect." He believes that "there is guidance," there is a "larger picture," a "vector of creation"—that our life experiment is "about something."[57]

Religious symbology is extremely important for Everett. As he expressed it to me: "Symbols are it!" His affinity with Kabbalah is manifest in his feeling that both the masculine and the

feminine—the Holy One, Blessed be He and the *Shechina*—are
necessary to express the idea of a personal God. Thus, Everett ad-
vocates that on the High Holy Days, we offer our prayers to "Our
Father, our King; our Mother, our Queen."

Prayer, to Everett, is a process of judging and joining. The
Hebrew word for prayer, *Tefila*, derives from the root
"pallel"—"to judge." So, prayer for Gendler involves a sorting
out—a judgment—of those possibilities that rightly invite our care,
our concern. Gendler also sees *Tefila* as related to the word
"petil"—a thread—denoting the connection of the self with the
Divine direction, flow or purpose. Prayer for Everett is thus, "a
clarified connection with the Divine."

Everett sees the *Sefirot* as a meaningful contemporary symbol.
He describes a personal meditative experience in which the ten
Sefirot represent the energy flow from above, as it permeates the
individual; or, put differently, the intellectual and emotional
aspects of the Divine as immanent in man.

Another meaningful symbol for Everett is the Eternal Light,
above the Holy Ark in the Temple. At the present time, Rabbi
Gendler serves as spiritual leader of Temple Emanuel in Lowell,
Massachusetts and is also Jewish chaplain at Phillips Academy in
Andover, Massachusetts. At the Lowell synagogue, Gendler has
designed what may be the first solar powered Eternal Light in a
Temple. The *Boston Evening Globe* described Everett's innovation
and the dedication of his solar-run Eternal Light:

> It grew from his musings about light and the sun, "how the sun is a
> symbol of divine power, and the way it sustains us," he recalled. That
> led to thoughts about diminishing petroleum supplies, nuclear pollu-
> tion and even how the traditional fuel of an Eternal Light, olive oil, is
> the product of a natural solar-energy collector, an olive tree. "Symbol-
> ically it seemed logical to establish a closer relationship to the sun,"
> Gendler said, "and I had heard about photovoltaic cells."
>
> These cells, first developed to turn sunlight into electricity aboard
> spacecraft, are undergoing development by universities and a number
> of private enterprises, including at least three subsidiaries of major oil
> companies, in an effort to reduce their price.

Through electrochemistry, they capture the sun's rays and convert them into tiny amounts of power which can be stored in batteries for later use. . . .

In tonight's service, Gendler plans to first light a traditional olive oil lamp, then use handrolled beeswax candles to light a seven-branch menorah, and only then turn on the solar-powered Eternal Light.

The sequence of these different forms of energy, he said, is meant to be symbolic of the stages of illumination of human lives, both physically and spiritually.[58]

The creation of new and contemporary forms is thus another option for the modern questing Jew.

In addition to a renewed emphasis on nature mysticism, and a more inclusive religious symbology, what other options does Gendler suggest? A very significant one in which Everett Gendler has played an important role is the *havurah*. In 1968, in Somerville, Massachusetts, in a yellow frame house on College Avenue a few miles from Cambridge, Havurat Shalom was inaugurated. Havurat Shalom was an experiment that marked a new direction for American Jewry.

The idea of a havurah did not begin with this Boston group.[59] More than six years previous to the founding of Havurat Shalom, Jacob Neusner spoke about *havurot* (fellowships) which existed in Talmudic times, and recommended their application to our time. The Reconstructionist movement had also promoted the concept of *havurot*. Accordingly, we find an excellent introduction to the concept of the *havurah* in the Reconstructionist pamphlet *The Havurah Idea* by Jacob Neusner and Ira Eisenstein.[60] In this pamphlet, the *havurah* is defined as "a Jewish study and action fellowship. It is composed of a small group of men and women who share certain concerns and commitments. The members of a *havurah* think and act together to advance their commitments and to further Jewish life as a whole."[61]

What is the significance of the term "fellowship"? How, for example, does "fellowship" differ from "friendship"? Neusner points out that "friendship involves two people—fellowship, two people and one ideal held in common."[62] Fellowship, Neusner continues, "is predicated on a common goal or ideal shared among two or more people, drawing them together despite, not because of, their particularities and uniqueness."[63]

Ira Eisenstein, President of the Reconstructionist Rabbinical College, sees the member of a *havurah* as not merely a nominal Jew—paying dues to a Jewish organization—but as a committed Jew. The *havurah* in action, for Eisenstein, is a small group that provides a design for intimate Jewish living. He writes: "Since the *havurah* should serve as a vehicle for intimate, Jewish living, it should give its members an opportunity to experience the joys of Shabbat and Yom Tov in an informal, warm atmosphere. Families should come together to sing, to play music, to dance, to read and to worship."[64]

Now that the basic concept of the *havurah* is clear, we ask: how was this implemented at Havurat Shalom in Boston? The moving force behind Havurat Shalom was Rabbi Arthur Green.[65] Green was particularly troubled by the fact that many young religious seekers found nothing of value in Judaism. Green himself has always been a seeker, with strong mystical inclinations and a fascination with Kabbalah and Hasidism. His interest was more in experimenting with the full range of religious tradition rather than in maintaining the strict line of halakhah—Jewish law.[66]

Arthur Green is now assistant professor of Religion at the University of Pennsylvania and the author of the highly acclaimed book *Tormented Master: A Life of Rabbi Nahman of Bratslav.*[67] During the recent visit of Arthur Green to the University of Rhode Island, I had an opportunity to discuss with him the original concept of the *havurah* in which he played such a definitive role. Green defined his concept of a *havurah* in this manner: "A *havurah* is a small group of Jews seriously seeking a Jewish religious life-style appropriate to themselves in the context of community."[68] What is the role of mysticism in the *havurah*? Green spoke of the need to integrate mystical "highs" into the daily life of the Jew. In this vein he has written: "We do not always live in the glow of spiritual shabbos. When we don't, we have to begin from below. . . . The discovery of the Presence in the world below, in the very earthiness of the weekday, then becomes our task."[69]

The search for the presence of God within the world is one factor that motivated Arthur Green and those associated with him to foster the *havurah* movement. (Green pointed out that he is presently involved in an alternative minyan in Philadelphia—a type of *havurah*—and he also made mention of the New York *Havurah*. There are also *havurot* now within the framework of many synagogues. Our concern here is with those *havurot* not involved with the synagogue, whose members have mystical, devotional, and spiritual interests.) Among those who were involved with Arthur Green in the initial stages of Havurat Shalom in Somerville were Zalman Schachter and Everett Gendler.

Zalman Schachter, professor of Religion at Temple University, teaches Jewish mysticism and general psychology and religion. He is an ordained Lubavicher Rabbi. Whenever I have been with him, I have always been impressed with the earnestness of his spiritual quest. In an essay he wrote about mystical prayer, I noticed a dramatic instance of his preoccupation with the spirit. He wrote that at a certain crucial point in his life, he had the good fortune to meet Howard Thurman, then Dean of the Chapel at Boston University. Schachter wrote: "In our first meeting he floored me with the question: 'Don't you believe in the Holy Spirit?' But he said it in Hebrew, *Ruach Hakodesh*. I left his office and spent three weeks living through hell, trying to figure out if I did indeed trust God."[70] This self-examination to determine if he really did surrender his life to God is characteristic of Zalman.

It is interesting to note that in his discussion of the *havurah*, Everett Gendler, too, emphasized the search for the spiritual. Everett Gendler defines a *havurah* as an "alternative Jewish religious community," i.e., an alternative to the larger communities represented by synagogues and Jewish community centers. *Havurot* are relatively small groups (10 to 35 people) striving for an authentic and integrated Jewish lifestyle.[71] Everett presently participates in such an alternative Jewish religious community in Marblehead, Massachusetts. In addition to its emphasis on the intimacy between its members and the activity of all its members, the *havurah*—in Gendler's view—is primarily "a kind of vessel that more directly receives the spirit."[72]

Recall the early influence of the Quakers on Everett Gendler's religious development. Gendler sees a Quaker-like motif in the *havurah*, for as Gendler puts it, the *havurah* involves "a small, more intimate, less structured unit that makes a place for expressions of the spirit—not unlike a Quaker meeting."[73] Herein, for Gendler, lies the spiritual significance of the *havurah* movement. In an intriguing statement, similar to the provocative question Dean Thurman asked Zalman Schachter, Gendler said to me, "The Spirit is not entirely under our control; spiritual reality cannot be totally prescribed."[74] In a small, intimate group such as a *havurah*, there is a greater openness to the Spirit. In Gendler's pointed words lies the answer to Dean Thurman's question about belief in the Holy Spirit. Gendler said: *"Ruach Hakodesh*—the Holy Spirit—is still here."[75]

In Gendler's description of a service at Havurat Shalom, we can see how its members are particularly open to the channels of spiritual reality:

What is it about the *Havurah* service that makes it so appealing? Is it the informal seating arrangement, with cushions placed on the floor in somewhat random but finally circular fashion? Is it the intimacy of the small room? With sliding doors open, three rooms can form to accomodate perhaps 80 persons, but it's a squeeze, and no one feels lost in vast or pretentious space.

The leader of the service that morning sits on the floor, along with everyone else, and most likely begins with a *nigun*, a melody, usually wordless and usually from the hasidic or neo-hasidic repertoire. Those present soon join in, and if the melody chosen by the leader corresponds to or can capture the moods of those present, bodies may begin swaying, the *nigun* may go on for some minutes, rise to a crescendo, then taper off into meditative silence. On the other hand, it may catch on only feebly, in which case it is soon ended and another begun, or perhaps after a period of silence some words of the traditional prayer book will follow.

As the service proceeds, there will likely be interpolations of the leader: sometimes very personal comments about what the prayer means to him or her (yes, women lead the service also, though less frequently than men), sometimes a selection of poetry which is deeply

felt, sometimes another *nigun* to carry wordlessly the spirit of a particular passage beyond the verbal level.[76]

"The spirit of a particular passage beyond the verbal level"—it is
this emphasis on the spirit that marks the *havurah* as a contemporary option for the Jew in search of a mystical approach to
Judaism.

There was one other contemporary option that Everett Gendler
mentioned to me, one whose relationship to mysticism was not
immediately evident. Rabbi Gendler has long been active in civil
rights, the peace movement and ecumenicism. How are these
social action concerns relevant to the mystical quest? Gendler told
me about a poignant incident in his life that points up the connection dramatically.

In August, 1962, Everett Gendler was jailed in Albany, Georgia
as a result of his civil rights activities there. The late Rabbi
Abraham Joshua Heschel, Professor of Jewish Mysticism and
Ethics at the Jewish Theological Seminary, sent Gendler a
telegram which included the Biblical verse from Isaiah: "The God
of holiness is sanctified through righteousness," and these words of
Heschel: "Nothing is deeper than the craving for righteousness
and justice."[77]

Judaism has a world-affirming—not a world-negating—mysticism. The experience of God can include the affirmation of one's
fellow man as God's creature—and the making of a better world
for all through social action.

Reflection

Mysticism in Judaism is no mere solitary quest. In each human
"thou," Buber wrote, we perceive the "Eternal Thou." Contemporary Jewish mysticism is not merely an ascent "heavenward" to
attain an experience of spirituality. It also involves bringing
spiritual insights down to earth and applying them to concrete
situations. A mystical experience of cosmic unity, such as Rav
Kook's, can give rise to the ethical concept of the universal
brotherhood of all mankind; the unity of all peoples.

In Judaism, therefore, the mystical experience involves both heaven and earth, both God and man. The need to discover God in the context of our relations with our fellow human beings on earth as well as in spiritual ascents to "heaven" is underscored in these poetic words:

> And, if you ask me of God, my God
> "Where is He that in joy we may worship Him?"
> Here on earth too He lives, not in heaven alone,
> And this earth He has given to man.[78]

Epilogue: Gateways to God

The Hasidic Rabbi Menahem Mendel of Kotzk said: "God sends souls down to earth and then brings them back by making them climb ladders. Thence man's preoccupation: souls upon souls, all in pursuit of ladders."[1]

If we look deeply into our own souls, we may discover a "sixth sense", an intuitive feeling that there is more to our existence than our brief life-span on earth. The poet William Wordsworth wrote:

> Our birth is but a sleep and a forgetting:
> The soul that rises with us, our life's star,
> Hath had elsewhere its setting,
> And cometh from afar:
> Not in entire forgetfulness,
> And not in utter nakedness,
> But trailing clouds of glory do we come
> From God, who is our home.[2]

In this book we have seen the tracing of a series of journeys and a retracing of our footsteps back to God, who is our home. Those who wish to take the journey themselves may ask, "What are the gateways to God, what ladders do we climb?"

We began by inviting the reader to take the first step on the longest journey: the journey inwards. Remember the suggestive words of Dag Hammarskjold:

> The longest journey is the journey inwards
> Of him who has chosen his destiny,
> Who has started upon his quest
> For the source of his being.[3]

These words of Hammarskjold indicate a gateway to God: *inward meditation.* This kind of meditation involves the whole self; it is a looking within, a search for the source of our being. Through meditation, we realize that we are more than machines or human computers who think, more than flesh and blood, more than intelligent organisms. We are souls. We have within us an immortal aspect akin to God, by which we can attain to knowledge of God. There is another kind of knowing besides the scientific way, intuitive knowledge of the soul.

Such knowledge is immediate and direct. It binds us to the universe. It gives us a feeling of belonging to the cosmos, to ultimate reality, to God. It is above all a feeling of unity, a sense of the interconnectedness of all things. A dialogue between a student and his teacher of meditation expresses the nature of this knowledge:

> "I see that everything which happens is reflected in everything else."
>
> "Yes," the master said. "Anything else?"
>
> "I see that every action of any man has its result in all other men, and not only in all men, but in all beings, and in all spheres."
>
> "Anything else?"
>
> "Everything is connected with everything."⁴

The deeper we meditate upon our inner selves, the more we come to feel the psychic unity of mankind, and the more certainly we know that we belong here—we are part of that universal process which connects everything with everything else. This is the gateway of inward meditation.

Contemplation, or outward meditation, deep concentration on something external to ourselves is another gateway to God, another ladder of infinity. Contemplate a grain of sand, a flower, a brook, a tree—an act of contemplation can give us a sense of the unity of all things. Our oneness with the universe is reflected in these immortal words:

> *To see the world in a grain of sand*
> *And a heaven in a wild flower,*

Hold infinity in the palm of your hand
And eternity in an hour.[5]

The mystical experience, we begin to realize, is open to all. One does not have to be a practicing religionist to experience oneness. What is needed is to be open to the act of experiencing itself. The gateways to God are contemplation, meditation, and knowledge—the ineffable knowledge of the oneness of the universe in God.

Jewish mysticism utilizes these gateways to God, contemplation, meditation, and knowledge, but adds its own unique symbols, its own unique journeys, its own unique ladders:

> Jewish mysticism in its various forms represents an attempt to interpret the religious values of Judaism in terms of mystical values. It concentrates upon the idea of the living God who manifests himself in the acts of Creation, Revelation and Redemption. Pushed to its extreme, the mystical meditation on this idea gives birth to the conception of a sphere, a whole realm of divinity, which underlies the world of our sense-data and which is present and active in all that exists. This is the meaning of what the Kabbalists call the world of the *Sefiroth.*[6]

The *Sefirot* are Jewish mystical symbols of the omnipresence of God. They are, we recall, the ten aspects through which the hidden God—*Ein-Sof*—manifests Himself; the ten powers or attributes of God; the "stages through which the divine life pulsates back and forth."[7] And here indeed lies the provocative power of Jewish mysticism. It is not only man who embarks on a mystical journey to God. God, in Jewish mysticism, is conceived of as having an inner life. There is an inner journey that takes place within God! One aspect of this journey, in the Jewish religious consciousness, is God's turning to man.

Judah Halevi, the medieval Jewish poet and philosopher who inclined toward mysticism, expressed this daring theological concept in these words:

Lord, where shall I find Thee?
High and hidden in Thy place;
And where shall I not find Thee?
The world is full of Thy glory.
I have sought Thy nearness;
With all my heart have I called Thee,
And going out to meet Thee
I found Thee coming toward me.[8]

As man (man is used here in a generic sense to signify both men
and women) ascends the ladder toward God, he discovers that
God is descending the ladder to meet him. In addition to contemplation, meditation, and knowledge there is a fourth gateway
to God in Jewish mysticism, love: love of man for God and love
radiating from God to man. There is a constant flow of energy, of
love, up and down the ladder—the ladder between heaven and
earth, God and man.

In Judaism, God's love for man is expressed by His gift of the
Torah; man's love for God is expressed by his study of Torah and
in his observance of God's commandments. An especially
beautiful Jewish book of love is the Biblical *Song of Songs,* said by
the Rabbis to express the love between the Jewish people and
God.

But the love of man for God must also be expressed in terms of
man's love for his fellow human beings. Jewish spirituality is not
simply a dialogue between the individual and God. It is a fusing of
many souls in community. And it involves making this earth a better place in which to live. In Jewish mysticism, the ultimate goal of
the love between man and God is *tikkun*—mending the world,
improving mankind, making earth more like heaven.

And so, the four elements of Jewish mysticism are all intercon-
nected: Heaven and Earth, God and Man. They are all a
unity—within God. As a parent transcends a child, so God
transcends the universe. But as characteristics of the parent are
present in the child, so God is immanent in the universe.

The Psalmist best expresses the Jewish conception of the

omnipresence of God, upon which the Jewish mystics expand:

Whither shall I go from Thy spirit?
Or whither shall I flee from Thy presence?

If I ascend up into heaven, Thou art there;
If I make my bed in the netherworld behold, Thou art there.

If I take the wings of the morning,
And dwell in the uttermost parts of the sea;

Even there would Thy right hand lead me,
And Thy right hand would hold me. . . .

I will give thanks unto Thee, for I am fearfully
and wonderfully made;

Wonderful are Thy works;
And that my soul knoweth right well.[9]

Heaven, Earth and Man—held together in Unity by a loving embrace of God—this is the final destination of all Jewish mystical journeys.

Notes

NOTES TO INTRODUCTION

¹*The Prayer Book: Weekday, Sabbath and Festival*, translated and arranged by Ben Zion Bokser (New York: Hebrew Publishing Company, 1957), p. 19.
²Gershom G. Scholem, *On the Kabbalah and Its Symbolism*, trans. Ralph Mannheim (New York: Schocken Books, 1969), p. 5.
³William Blake, *"Auguries of Innocence,"* in *William Blake: The Complete Poems* edited by Alicia Ostriker (New York: Penguin Books, 1977), p. 506.
⁴Arthur Darby Nock, *St. Paul,* (New York: Harper Torchbooks, 1963, p. 66.
⁵See Reynold A. Nicholson, *The Mystics of Islam* (New York: Schocken Books, 1975), p. 5.
⁶Mishnah Sotah 9:15, trans. Herbert Danby in *The Mishnah* (London: Oxford University Press, 1933), pp. 306, 307.
⁷Bahya Ben Joseph Ibn Pakuda, *The Book of Direction to the Duties of the Heart*, translated from the Arabic and edited by Menahem Mansoor (London: Routledge and Kegan Paul, 1973). The description of the contents of this classic is based on this edition.
⁸Dag Hammarskjold, *Markings*, trans. Leif Sjoberg and W. H. Auden (New York: Alfred A. Knopf, 1964), p. 58.
⁹Mircea Eliade, *Shamanism: Archaic Techniques of Ecstasy*, trans. Willard R. Trask (New York: Pantheon Books, 1964), p. xix.
¹⁰See note 8, above.

NOTES TO CHAPTER 1

¹Ezekiel 1:1, *The Holy Scriptures* (Philadelphia: Jewish Publication Society, 1960), p. 644.
²Hannah Grad Goodman, *The Story of Prophecy* (New York: Behrman House, Inc., 1965), p. 188.
³Psalms 137, *The Holy Scriptures*, p. 874.
⁴Ezekiel 1:3, ibid, p. 644.
⁵*Ezekiel, Hebrew Text and English Translation*, commentary by S. Fisch (London: The Soncino Press, 1950), p. 2.
⁶Mortimer J. Cohen, *Pathways Through The Bible* (Philadelphia: Jewish Publication Society, 1959), pp. 402, 403.
⁷Ezekiel 1:28, *The Holy Scriptures*, p. 644.
⁸Ibid.
⁹For the interpretation of Ezekiel's vision of God and his response to the theophany, I am indebted to Professor Nahum Sarna of Brandeis University for his helpful suggestions.

[1]See Max L. Margolis and Alexander Marx, *A History of the Jewish People* (Philadelphia: Jewish Publication Society, 1947), pp. 189-195.

[2]See Hans Jonas, *The Gnostic Religion* (Boston: Beacon Press, 1958). For the influence of Gnosticism on Jewish mysticism, see Gershom G. Scholem, *Jewish Gnosticism, Merkabah Mysticism and Talmudic Tradition* (New York: The Jewish Theological Seminary of America, 1965).

[3]Quoted in Gershom Scholem, *Major Trends in Jewish Mysticism* (New York: Schocken Books, 1947), p. 49.

[4]Milton Steinberg, *As a Driven Leaf* (New York: Behrman House, 1939), p. 186.

[5]See Louis Finkelstein, *Akiba* (Philadelphia: Jewish Publication Society, 1936). p. 6.

[6]Ethics of the Fathers, 4:2 from *Sayings of the Fathers*, Hertz Edition, (New York: Behrman House, 1945), p. 69.

[7]Babylonian Talmud, *Hagigah* 14b, translation based on Allen Unterman, *The Wisdom of the Mystics* (New York: A New Directions Book, 1976), p. 29. For the complete text from the Talmud, see Appendix II, p. 199.

[8]See Scholem, *Jewish Gnosticism*, p. 14.

[9]Exodus 33:20, *The Holy Scriptures* (Philadelphia: Jewish Publication Society 1960), p. 107

[10]Babylonian Talmud, *Hagigah* 15b (London: The Soncino Press, 1938).

[1]See Seymour Rossel, *When a Jew Seeks Wisdom* (New York: Behrman House, 1975), p. 38.

[2]Daniel 12:2, 3, *Holy Scriptures*, pg. 1146.

[3]Raymond A. Moody, Jr., *Life After Life* (New York: Bantam Books, 1976), pp. 58, 59.

[4]*Zohar: The Book of Splendor*, selected and edited by Gershom Scholem (New York: Schocken Books, 1963), p. 28.

[5]Babylonian Talmud, *Shabbath* 33b.

[6]See Scholem, *Major Trends*, fifth lecture, pp. 156-204.

[7]See ibid., pp. 186, 187.

[8]Ibid., pp. 190, 191.

[9]Meyer Waxman, *A History of Jewish Literature*, vol. 2 (New York: Thomas Yoseloff, 1933), pp. 392, 393.

[10]See Scholem's introduction to *Zohar: The Book of Splendor*, p. 7.

[11]See Bernard Martin, *A History of Judaism*, vol. II (New York: Basic Books, 1974), p. 40.

[12]*The Zohar*, trans. Harry Sperling and Maurice Simon (London: The Soncino Press, 1933), vol. II, pp. 109, 110.

[13]Ibid., vol. III 92a-92b.

¹⁴For the influence of this medieval concept on the *Kabbalah*, see David Wolf Silverman, "Animadversions on the Mystical Turn," in *Conservative Judaism* (Summer 1976) pp. 29, 30.
¹⁵*Zohar: The Book of Splendor*, pp. 91-94.
¹⁶*The Zohar*, vol. IV, pp. 219, 220.
¹⁷See Israel Levinthal, *Judaism: An Analysis and an Interpretation* (New York: Funk and Wagnalls, 1935), chapters 9 and 10.

NOTES TO CHAPTER 4

¹Gershom Scholem, *Kabbalah* (New York: The New York Times Book Co., 1974), pp. 99, 100.
²See Gershom Scholem, *Major Trends*, p. 206.
³See Gershom Scholem, *Kabbalah*, p. 100.
⁴Babylonian Talmud, *Hagigah* 12b.
⁵Scholem, *Kabbalah*, p. 102.
⁶Abraham J. Heschel, *The Mystical Element in Judaism*, p. 934.
⁷See Scholem, *Major Trends*, p. 217.
⁸*Midrash Rabbah* on *Exodus*, trans. S. M. Lehrman (London: The Soncino Press, 1961), 28:5, p. 335.
⁹Ibid., 29:1, p. 337.
¹⁰Scholem, *Kabbalah*, p. 105 (quotation from *Ma'arekhet ha Elohut*).
¹¹Gershom Scholem, *Kabbalah*, p. 109. Scholem states that this *Sefirah* also represents nothingness. My interpretation of the *Sefirot* is based largely on Scholem, *Kabbalah* and *Major Trends*.
¹²For this insight, I am indebted to Rabbi James B. Rosenberg.
¹³See *Midrash Rabbah*, *Genesis*, Parashat Vayera.
¹⁴See Perle Epstein, *Kabbalah: The Way of the Jewish Mystic* (New York: Doubleday, 1978), pp. 57, 58.
¹⁵*Zohar, The Book of Splendor*, p. 78.

NOTES TO CHAPTER 5

¹Yoma 6:2 in *The Mishnah: Oral Teachings of Judaism*, selected and translated by Eugene J. Lipman (New York: Schocken Books, 1974), p. 116.
²Exodus 3:14.
³For Abulafia's biography, I have consulted Scholem, *Major Trends*, and Epstein, *Kabbalah: The Way of the Mystic.*
⁴Scholem, *Major Trends*, p. 131.
⁵*Cf.* Lawrence Kushner, *The Book of Letters* (New York: Harper and Row, 1975), pp. 4, 5.
⁶*Avodah Zarah* 8a, quoted in ibid., p. 4.
⁷*Exodus Rabbah* on Parashat Vayakhel, quoted in ibid., p. 5.
⁸Perle Epstein, *Kabbalah: The Way of the Jewish Mystic*, pp.96, 97.

[9]Scholem, *Major Trends*, pp. 142.
[10]Genesis 1:27. *The Holy Scriptures*, p. 5.

NOTES TO CHAPTER 6

[1]See Max L. Margolis and Alexander Marx, *A History of the Jewish People*, pp. 470-472.
[2]Gershom Scholem, *Kabbalah*, p. 420.
[3]See Perle Epstein, *Kabbalah: The Way of the Jewish Mystic*, p. 19.
[4]See Solomon Schechter, "Safed in the Sixteenth Century," in his *Studies in Judaism* (Philadelphia: Jewish Publication Society, 1958), pp. 231-297.
[5]Ibid., p. 259.
[6]Epstein, pp. 17, 18.
[7]Bernard S. Raskas, *Heart of Wisdom* (New York: The Burning Bush Press), p. 222.
[8]See Midrash, *Bereshis Rabba* to Genesis 1:5 and 1:31.
[9]See Martin Buber, *Hasidism and Modern Man*, trans. Maurice Friedman (New York: Harper Torchbooks, 1966), p. 216.
[10]Buber, ibid.
[11]Ibid.
[12]Ibid.
[13]Gershom Scholem, *Sabbatai Zevi*, p. 34.
[14]Buber, ibid.
[15]Scholem, p. 46.

NOTES TO CHAPTER 7

[1]See Samuel Hugo Bergman, *Faith and Reason*, trans. Alfred Jospe (New York: Schocken Books, 1963), p. 128, where the author cites Rabbi Abraham Isaac Kook's positive attitude toward Darwin's theory. Rabbi Kook, who was chief Rabbi of Israel, was a twentieth century Jewish mystic.
[2]Genesis 1:26, 27, *The Holy Scriptures*.
[3]Genesis 2:7, *The Holy Scriptures*.
[4]See Seymour Rossel, *When a Jew Seeks Wisdom* (New York: Behrman House, 1973), p. 46.
[5]*Sifre Deuteronomy* 306:132a. See also Seymour Rossel, ibid., for an interpretation of this passage.
[6]Martin Buber, *The Way of Man: According to the Teaching of Hasidism* (New York: The Citadel Press, 1966), p. 12.
[7]See Seymour Rossel, chapter 3, for a clear and concise explanation of the meaning of *Yetzer HaRa*.
[8]Psalm 8:4-7, my translation.
[9]*Mishnah Sanhedrin* 4:5
[10]See Gershom Scholem, *Sabbatai Sevi: The Mystical Messiah* (Princeton: Princeton University Press, 1973), p.38.

[11]*Mishnah Sanhedrin*.

[12]*Zohar* 1:24b. Soncino edition. See Seymour Rossel's treatment of this passage, p. 24.

[13]Abraham J. Heschel, "The Mystical Element in Judaism" in *The Jews: Their History, Religion and Culture*, edited by Louis Finkelstein (Philadelphia: Jewish Publication Society, 1960), vol. II, p. 935.

[14]Ibid.

[15]Abraham J. Heschel, *Who Is Man?* (Stanford: Stanford University Press, 1965), p. 24.

NOTES TO CHAPTER 8

[1]See Joseph Klausner, *The Messianic Idea in Israel*, trans. W. F. Stinespring (New York: The Macmillan Company, 1965).

[2]Isaiah 53:3-5.

[3]*A Curriculum For The Afternoon Jewish School* (New York: United Synagogue, 1978), p. 635.

[4]See Gershom Scholem, *Sabbatai Sevi: the Mystical Messiah*, trans. R. J. Zwi Werblowsky (Princeton: Princeton University Press, 1973), p. 104.

[5]Quoted in Scholem, *Major Trends*, pp. 294, 295.

NOTES TO CHAPTER 9

[1]Martin Buber, *Tales of the Hasidim: Early Masters* (New York: Schocken Books, 1947), p. 12.

[2]Aryeh Rubinstein, *Hasidism* (New York: Leon Amiel, 1975), p. 10.

[3]*Ethics of the Fathers* 2:6. Hertz edition, p. 33.

[4]Elie Wiesel, *Souls on Fire* (New York: Random House, 1972), p. 25.

[5]Jerome R. Mintz, *Legends of the Hasidim* (Chicago: The University of Chicago Press, 1968), pp. 7, 8.

[6]Buber, *Tales of the Hasidim: Early Masters*, p. 66.

[7]Buber, ibid., p. 107.

[8]Scholem, *Major Trends*, pp. 333, 334.

[9]Buber, *Tales*, p. 53.

[10]Wiesel, p. 26.

[11]Buber, p. 52.

[12]Ibid., p. 51.

[13]Martin Buber, *Hasidism and Modern Man*, ed. and trans. Maurice Friedman (New York: Harper Torchbooks, 1966), p. 49.

[14]See Rubinstein, p. 22.

NOTES TO CHAPTER 10

[1]Aryeh Rubinstein, *Hasidism* (New York: Leon Amiel, 1975), p. 22.

[2]Samuel H. Dresner, *The Zaddik* (New York: Abelard Schuman, 1960), p. 48.
[3]Ibid., pp. 38-40.
[4]Martin Buber, *Tales of the Hasidim*, p. 5.
[5]Elie Wiesel, *Souls on Fire*, p. 71.
[6]Martin Buber, *Tales*, pp. 212, 213.
[7]Martin Buber, *The Tales of Rabbi Nachman*, trans. Maurice Friedman (Bloomington: Indiana University Press, 1962), pp. 24, 25.
[8]Ibid., p. 26.
[9]Seymour Rossel, *When a Jew Seeks Wisdom* (New York: Behrman House, 1975), p. 56.
[10]Ibid., p. 54. See also Martin Buber, *Hasidism and Modern* Man, p. 140.

NOTES TO CHAPTER 11

[1]Elie Wiesel, *Souls On Fire*, p. 30.
[2]Abraham J. Heschel, *Man's Quest for God* (New York: Charles Scribner's Sons), pp. 49, 50, 52.
[3]Jiri Langer, *Nine Gates to the Chassidic Mysteries*, translated by Stephen Jolly (New York: Behrman House, 1976), pp. 5-8.
[4]Martin Buber, *Hasidism and Modern Man*, pp. 50-53.
[5]Ibid., p. 52.
[6]Ibid.
[7]Jerome R. Mintz, *Legends of the Hasidim* p. 33.
[8]Richard Siegel, Michael Strassfeld, and Sharon Strassfeld, *The Jewish Catalog* (Philadelphia: Jewish Publication Society, 1973), p. 288.
[9]Ibid., p. 285.
[10]Ibid.
[11]Ibid., pp. 285-288. The address of the Lubavicher Hasidim central headquarters is 770 Eastern Parkway, Brooklyn, New York.
[12]Personal interview with Rabbi Yehoshua Laufer, representative of the Lubavicher Hasidic movement in Providence, R. I., December 5, 1979.
[13]George Woodcock, *Thomas Merton* (New York: Farrar, Straus, Giroux, 1978), p. 99.
[14]Wiesel, *Souls on Fire*, p. 26.
[15]*Challenge: An Encounter with Lubavich—Chabad* (published by the Lubavich Foundation of Great Britain), p. 189.
[16]Psalms 35:10. *The Holy Scriptures*.
[17]For more information on the significance of Hasidic dancing, see *Challenge*, pp. 195-201.
[18]*Challenge*, p. 282.
[19]Ibid., pp. 286, 287.
[20]Ibid., p. 304.
[21]Personal interview with Rabbi Levi Yitzchak Horowitz (the Bostoner Rebbe), December 27, 1979.
[22]Ibid.

[1]Martin Buber, *Hasidism and Modern Man*, p. 53.
[2]Grete Schneder, *The Hebrew Humanism of Martin Buber*, trans. Noah J. Jacobs (Detroit: Wayne State University Press, 1973), p. 27.
[3]Ibid., p. 28.
[4]Aubrey Hodes, *Martin Buber: An Intimate Portrait* (New York: The Viking Press, 1971), p. 45.
[5]Martin Buber, *Between Man and Man*, trans. Ronald Gregor Smith (New York: The Macmillan Co., 1965), pp. 22, 23.
[6]David Johnson, program notes to *Gustav Mahler: Symphony No. 3 in D Minor*, New York Philharmonic, Leonard Bernstein, conductor, Columbia Records
[7]Buber, *Between Man and Man*, p. 136.
[8]Ibid., pp. 136, 137.
[9]Buber, *Hasidism and Modern Man*, pp. 56, 57.
[10]Ibid., p. 57.
[11]Robert E. Wood, *Martin Buber's Ontology* (Evanston, Illinois: Northwestern University Press, 1969), p. 6.
[12]Buber, *Hasidism and Modern Man*, p. 59.
[13]Ibid., pp. 74, 77, 78.
[14]Martin Buber, *Meetings*, edited with an introduction by Maurice Friedman (Lasalle, Illinois: Open Court, 1973), p. 10.
[15]Buber, *Hasidism and Modern Man*, p. 49.
[16]Martin Buber, *I and Thou*, trans. Ronald Gregor Smith (New York: Charles Scribner's Sons, 1958), pp. 80, 81.
[17]Martin Buber, *At The Turning*, p. 44.
[18]*Orot*, "Lights," is a collection of essays, some of which were published separately in journals or in booklet form. The earliest edition was published in Jerusalem in 1925 under the auspices of *Degel Yerushalayim* ("The Banner of Jerusalem"), a movement Rabbi Kook launched to further his own philosophy of Judaism.
[19]*Orot Hateshuvah*, "The Lights of Penitence," is Rav Kook's most popular work. The first edition appeared in 1925 in Jerusalem. The most recent edition was edited by Ben Zion Bokser and is referred to below in note 21.
[20]*Orot Hakodesh*, "The Lights of Holiness," Rav Kook's most significant work, consists of three volumes of meditations on the mystery of God and human life in a God-dominated universe. These volumes were published under the auspices of the Agudah Hehotzoat Sifre Harayah Kook in Jerusalem, the first two volumes in 1938, the third in 1950. The selection and construction of these volumes was the work of Rav Kook's disciple David Ha-Kohen. The most recent edition (Bokser) is referred to below.
[21]Abraham Isaac Kook, *The Lights of Penitence, The Moral Principles, Lights of Holiness, Essays, Letters and Poems*, translation and introduction by Ben Zion Bokser, preface by Jacob Agus and Rivka Schatz (New York and Ramsey, N. J.: Paulist Press, 1978), p. 201.
[22]Ibid., p. 135.

[23]Ibid., p. 232.

[24]Abraham Isaac Kook, "The Experience of Mysticism," in *Contemporary Jewish Thought: A Reader*, edited with introductory notes by Simon Noveck (New York: B'nai B'rith Department of Adult Jewish Education, 1963), p. 99.

[25]Jacob Agus, *Banner of Jerusalem: The Life, Times and Thought of Abraham Isaac Kook* (New York: Bloch Publishing Co., 1946), p. 3. We have used this volume as our main source on Rav Kook's life.

[26]Ibid., p. 9.

[27]Ibid., p. 19.

[28]Ibid., p. 75.

[29]Ibid., p. 114.

[30]Kook, *The Lights of Penitence*, pp. 264, 265.

[31]See note 24 above.

[32]Agus, p. 125.

[33]Ibid., p. 126.

[34]Kook, *Zikkaron*, p. 16, cited in Agus, p. 132.

[35]Kook, *The Lights of Penitence*, p. 85.

[36]Kook, *Lights of Penitence*, p. 460, cited by Agus, p. 136.

[37]Sir James Jean, "A Great Thought," from *The Mysterious Universe* (Cambridge: Cambridge University Press). Italics added.

[38]Fritjof Capra, *The Tao of Physics* (New York: Bantam Books, 1977), p. 117.

[39]Bokser, p. 222.

[40]Ibid., p. 221.

[41]Ibid., pp. 221, 222.

[42]Abraham Isaac Kook, *Olot Rayah*, ("The Offering of Rabbi Abraham Isaac Ha-Kohen Kook," a two volume work including the full text of the Daily, Sabbath, and Festival Prayer Book, the Passover Haggadah, and the Ethics of the Fathers, with a running commentary. The first volume contains an introductory section on the meaning of prayer and the life of piety), Introduction, p. 13, translated and cited by Agus, p. 217.

[43]Ibid., Italics added.

[44]William Blake, *Auguries of Innocence*.

[45]Gershom Scholem, *Sabbatai Sevi: The Mystical Messiah*, p. 283.

[46]Everett Gendler, "On the Judaism of Nature," in *The New Jews*, ed. James A. Sleeper and Alan L. Mintz (New York: Vintage Books, 1971), p. 233.

[47]Personal interview with Everett Gendler, Andover, Massachusetts, February 6, 1980.

[48]Gendler, "On the Judaism of Nature," in Sleeper and Mintz, p. 233.

[49]These quotations are from the personal interview cited above.

[50]Gendler, "On the Judaism of Nature," in Sleeper and Mintz, p. 235.

[51]Ibid., p. 236.

[52]Ibid., p. 239.

[53]Personal interview with Everett Gendler.

[54]Gendler, "On the Judaism of Nature," in Sleeper and Mintz, p. 241.

[55]Ibid., p. 237.

[56]Everett Gendler, "Some Nature Elements in Jewish Worship," quotation of poem by Rabbi Nachman of Bratslav (1772-1811), trans. Rabbi Shamai Kanter, privately published, pp. 59, 60.

⁵⁷These quotations are from the personal interview, cited above.
⁵⁸*Boston Evening Globe*, Friday, December 22, 1978, p. 12.
⁵⁹For the history of the *havurah*, I have found helpful Stephen C. Lerner, "The Havurot," *Conservative Judaism*, vol. 24, no. 3, pp. 2-15.
⁶⁰Jacob Neusner and Ira Eisenstein, *The Havurah Idea*, pamphlet (New York: The Reconstructionist Press).
⁶¹Ibid., p. 1.
⁶²Ibid., p. 3.
⁶³Ibid., p. 4.
⁶⁴Ibid., p. 13.
⁶⁵See Lerner, p. 5.
⁶⁶Ibid.
⁶⁷Arthur Green, *Tormented Master: A Life of Rabbi Nachman of Bratslav*. (University, Alabama: University of Alabama Press, 1979).
⁶⁸Personal interview with Arthur Green, Kingston, R.I., February 28, 1980.
⁶⁹Arthur Green, "After Itzik: Toward a Theology of Jewish Spirituality," in *The New Jews*, p. 199.
⁷⁰Zalman M. Schachter, "On Mystical — Empirical Jewish Prayer — a 'Rap'" in Jerry V. Diller, *Ancient Roots and Modern Meanings: A Contemporary Reader in Jewish Identity* (New York: Bloch Publishing Company, 1978), p. 187.
⁷¹See the essay "Alternative Jewish Communities: An Overview" by David M. Szonyi in ibid., p. 269 ff.
⁷²Personal interview with Everett Gendler.
⁷³Ibid.
⁷⁴Ibid.
⁷⁵Ibid.
⁷⁶Everett Gendler, "Old—New Ways in Jewish Worship," *Hadassah Magazine* (November 1972), p. 16.
⁷⁷Personal interview with Everett Gendler.
⁷⁸Poem by Saul Tchernichovsky (ca. 1900), trans. R. Cover, E. Gendler, and A. Porat, quoted by Gendler in *The New Jews*, p. 243.

NOTES TO EPILOGUE

¹Elie Wiesel, *Souls on Fire* p. 245.
²William Wordsworth, "Ode," in *Intimations of Immortality*.
³Hammarskjold, *Markings*, p. 58.
⁴Janivillem van de Wetering, *The Empty Mirror* (Boston: Houghton Mifflin Company, 1975), p. 123.
⁵William Blake, *Auguries of Innocence*.
⁶Scholem, *Major Trends*, pp. 10, 11.
⁷Ibid., p. 208.
⁸Selected poems of Jehudah Halevi, translated by N. Solomon. (Philadelphia: Jewish Publication Socicety, 1928), pp. 134,135. Italics added.
⁹Psalms 139:7-10, 14, in *The Holy Scriptures* (Philadelphia: Jewish Publication Society, 1960), pp. 875, 876.

Suggested Readings

A. General Books on Mysticism, Religion
And Related Subjects

Eliade, Mircea. *Myth and Reality*. Translated by Willard R. Trask. New York: Harper Torchbooks, 1963.

Greeley, Andrew M. *Ecstasy: A Way of Knowing*. Englewood Cliffs, New Jersey: Prentice-Hall, Inc., 1974.

Jonas, Hans. *The Gnostic Religion*. Boston: Beacon Press, 1958.

LeShan, Lawrence. *How to Meditate*. New York: Bantam Books, 1975.

Needleman, Jacob. *The New Religions*. New York: Doubleday, 1970.

Otto, Rudolph. *The Idea of the Holy*. Translated by John W. Harvey. New York: Oxford University Press, 1958.

Parrinder, Geoffrey. *Mysticism in the World's Religions*. New York: Oxford University Press, 1976.

Scharfstein, Ben-Ami. *Mystical Experience*. Baltimore: Penguin Books, Inc., 1974

Stace, Walter T. *The Teachings of the Mystics*. New York: Mentor Books, 1960.

Underhill, Evelyn. *Mysticism*. New York: E.P. Dutton Co., 1961.

White, John, ed. *The Highest State of Consciousness*. New York: Anchor Books, 1972.

Zaehner, R.C. *Zen, Drugs and Mysticism*. New York: Vintage Books, 1972.

B. Jewish Mysticism

Agus, Jacob. *High Priest of Rebirth*. New York: Bloch Publishing Company, 1946.

Altmann, Alexander. *Studies in Jewish Mysticism and Philosophy*. Ithaca: Cornell University Press, 1969.

Bloom, Harold. *Kabbalah and Criticism*. New York: The Seabury Press, 1975.

Buber, Martin. *Between Man and Man*. Translated by Ronald Gregor Smith. Boston: Beacon Press, 1961.

——————. *Hasidism and Modern Man*. Edited and translated by Maurice Friedman. New York: Harper Torchbooks, 1966.

——————. *I and Thou*. Translated by Ronald Gregor Smith. New York: Charles Scribner's Sons, 1958.

——————. *Tales of the Hasidim: Early Masters.* New York: Schocken Books, 1947.

——————. *Tales of the Hasidim: Later Masters.* New York: Schocken Books, 1947.

Dresner, Samuel H. *The Zaddik.* New York: Abelard-Schuman, 1960.

Epstein, Perle. *Kabbalah: The Way of the Jewish Mystic.* New York: Doubleday and Company, 1978.

Friedman, Maurice. *Martin Buber: The Life of Dialogue.* New York: Harper Torchbooks, 1955.

Heschel, Abraham Joshua. *A Passion for Truth.* New York: Farrar, Straus and Giroux, 1973.

Jacobs, Louis. *Hasidic Thought.* New York: Behrman House, 1976.

Martin, Bernard and Silver, Daniel Jeremy. *A History of Judaism.* 2 vols. New York: Basic Books, 1974.

Mintz, Jerome R. *Legends of the Hasidim.* Chicago: University of Chicago Press, 1968.

Schaya, Leo. *The Universal Meaning of the Kabbalah.* Baltimore: Penguin Books, 1973.

Schechter, Solomon. *Studies in Judaism.* Philadelphia: Jewish Publication Society, 1958.

Scholem, Gershom G. *Jewish Gnosticism, Merkabah Mysticism and Talmudic Tradition.* New York: Schocken Books, 1960.

——————. *Kabbalah.* New York: Quadrangle. The New York Times Book Co., 1974.

——————. *Major Trends in Jewish Mysticism.* New York: Schocken Books, 1961.

——————. *The Messianic Idea in Judaism.* New York: Schocken Books, 1971.

——————. *On Jews and Judaism in Crisis.* Edited by Werner J. Dannhauser. New York: Schocken Books, 1976.

——————. *On the Kabbalah and Its Symbolism.* Translated by Ralph Mannheim. New York: Schocken Books, 1965.

——————. *Sabbatai Sevi: The Mystical Messiah.* Translated by R.J. Zwi Werblowsky. Princeton: Princeton University Press, 1973.

——————. *Zohar: The Book of Splendor,* selected and edited. New York: Schocken Books, 1963.

Tishby, I. *Mishnat Ha-Zohar,* 2 vols. Jerusalem, 1961.

Weiner, Herbert. *9½ Mystics.* New York: Collier Books, 1971.

Werblowsky, R. J. Z. *Joseph Karo: Lawyer and Mystic.* New York: Oxford University Press, 1972.

Wiesel, Elie. *Souls on Fire,* New York: Random House, 1972.

The Zohar. Translated by Harry Sperling and Maurice Simon, with an introduction by Dr. J. Abelson. 5 vols. London: The Soncino Press, 1933.

APPENDIX I

EZEKIEL'S VISION OF GOD

(The complete passage from the Bible)

¹Now it came to pass in the thirtieth year, in the fourth month, in the fifth day of the month, as I was among the captives by the river Chebar that the heavens were opened, and I saw visions of God. ²In the fifth day of the month, which was the fifth year of king Jehoiachin's captivity, ³the word of the Lord came expressly unto Ezekiel the priest, the son of Buzi, in the land of the Chaldeans by the river Chebar; and the hand of the Lord was there upon him.

⁴And I looked, and, behold, a stormy wind came out of the north, a great cloud, with a fire flashing up, so that a brightness was round about it; and out of the midst thereof as the colour of electrum, out of the midst of the fire. ⁵And out of the midst thereof came the likeness of four living creatures. And this was their appearance: they had the likeness of a man. ⁶And every one had four faces, and every one of them had four wings. ⁷And their feet were straight feet; and the sole of their feet was like the sole of a calf's foot; and they sparkled like the colour of burnished brass. ⁸And they had the hands of a man under their wings on their four sides; and as for the faces and wings of them four, ⁹their wings were joined one to another; they turned not when they went; they went every one straight forward. ¹⁰As for the likeness of their faces, they had the face of a man; and they four had the face of a lion on the right side; and they four had the face of an ox on the left side; they four had also the face of an eagle. ¹¹Thus were their faces; and their wings were stretched upward; two wings of every one were joined one to another, and two covered their bodies. ¹²And they went every one straight forward; whither the spirit was to go, they went; they turned not when they went. ¹³As for the likeness of of the living creatures, their appearance was like coals of fire, burning like the appearance of torches; it flashed up and down among the living creatures; and there was brightness to the fire, and out of the fire went forth lightning. ¹⁴And the living creatures ran and returned as the appearance of a flash of lightning.

¹⁵Now as I beheld the living creatures, behold one wheel at the bottom hard by the living creatures, at the four faces thereof. ¹⁶The appearance of the wheels and their work was like unto the colour of a beryl; and they four had one likeness; and their appearance and their work was as it were a wheel within a wheel. ¹⁷When they went, they went toward their four sides; they turned not when they went. ¹⁸As for their rings, they were high and they were dreadful; and they four had their rings full of eyes round about. ¹⁹And when the living creatures went, the wheels went hard by them; and when the living creatures were lifted up from the bottom, the wheels were lifted up. ²⁰Whithersoever the spirit was to go, as the spirit was to go thither, so they went; and the wheels were lifted up beside them; for the spirit of the living creature was in the wheels. ²¹When those went, these went, and when those stood, these stood; and when those were lifted up from the earth, the wheels were lifted up beside them; for the spirit of the living creature was in the wheels.

²²And over the heads of the living creatures there was the likeness of a firmament, like the colour of the terrible ice, stretched forth over their heads above. ²³And under the firmament were their wings conformable the one to the other; this one of them had two which covered, and that one of them had two which covered, their bodies. ²⁴And when they went, I heard the noise of their wings like the noise of great waters, like the voice of the Almighty, a noise of tumult like the noise of a host; when they stood, they let down their wings. ²⁵For, when there was a voice above the firmament that was over their heads, as they stood, they let down their wings.

²⁶And above the firmament that was over their heads was the likeness of a throne, as the appearance of a sapphire stone; and upon the likeness of the throne was a likeness as the appearance of a man upon it above. ²⁷And I saw as the colour of electrum, as the appearance of fire round about enclosing it, from the appearance of his loins and upward; and from the appearance of his loins and downward I saw as it were the appearance of fire, and there was brightness round about him. ²⁸As the appearance of the bow that is in the cloud in the day of rain, so was the appearance of the brightness round about. This was the appearance of the likeness of the glory of the Lord. And when I saw it, I fell upon my face, and I heard a voice of one that spoke.*

*Ezekiel, Chapter 1, a translation by the Jewish Publication Society of America (Philadelphia: Jewish Publication Society, 1954).

APPENDIX II

THE JOURNEY OF THE FOUR RABBIS
TO HEAVEN

(The complete passage from the Talmud)

Our Rabbis taught: Four men entered the 'Garden' (Heaven), namely, Ben Azzai and Ben Zoma, *Aher* and Rabbi Akiba. Rabbi Akiba said to them: When you arrive at the stones of pure marble, say not, Water, water! For it is said: He that speaketh falsehood shall not be established before mine eyes (Psalm 101, Verse 7). Ben Azzai cast a look and died. Of him Scripture says: Precious in the sight of the Lord is the death of his saints (Psalm 116, Verse 15). Ben Zoma looked and became demented. Of him Scripture says: Hast thou found honey? Eat so much as is sufficient for thee, lest thou be filled therewith, and vomit it. (Proverbs 25, Verse 16). *Aher* mutilated the shoots. Rabbi Akiba departed unhurt.*

*Babylonian Talmud, *Hagigah 14b*, translated by Rabbi Dr. I. Epstein, (London: The Soncino Press, 1938).

Index

203

208